The Story and the Song

A Survey of
English Musical Plays,
1916-78

By the same authors:

The Compleat Astrologer
The Compleat Lover
The Natural History of the Chorus Girl
The Immortals

The Story and the Song

A Survey of
English Musical Plays, 1916-78

Derek and Julia Parker

CHAPPELL & COMPANY | ELM TREE BOOKS

Chappell & Company Limited
50 New Bond Street, London W1A 2BR

London Amsterdam Brussels Hamburg
Johannesburg Madrid Milan Paris
Stockholm Sydney Toronto Wellington
Zurich New York

in association with
Elm Tree Books Limited
57-59 Long Acre, London, WC2E 9JL

First Published 1979

ISBN 0 903443 25 2

Designed by Ron Jones

Photoset by Amos Typesetters Hockley Essex

Design and production in association with
Book Production Consultants
7 Brooklands Avenue Cambridge

To
our respective mothers-in-law,
to whom
the piano scores
of most of these musicals
will be as familiar
as our faces

Contents

List of Illustrations

Foreword

This book is a record of British operetta and musical comedy — or, if you like, British musicals — since 1916; roughly between the production of *Chu Chin Chow* at His Majesty's Theatre, and the production at the Prince Edward Theatre of the rock opera *Evita*.

Those three terms most commonly used to describe a play containing lyrics set to music are really synonymous: there is only a terminological difference between 'operetta', 'musical comedy' and 'musical'. Roughly, one might say that the first is continental, the second British and the third American.

But we use them differently. One would not think of describing *The Golden Moth* as anything but a musical comedy; but one would hesitate to use that term to describe *The Rocky Horror Show*. Yet *The Rocky Horror Show* has all the ingredients of a Gaiety musical comedy of 1909 – a silly story about a naive young couple beset by comic villains in a never-never land, set to easily accessible music in a contemporary idiom. The term 'operetta' is no longer commonly in use, except when one speaks of the works of Strauss or Offenbach – yet surely it could be applied with total accuracy to the bewitching American musical *A Little Night Music*, right in the tradition of Léhar and Kálmán?

One finds oneself inevitably using the terms in a semi-critical sense. *Bless the Bride*, for instance, while it may not conform strictly to one's idea of 'an operetta', seems to deserve that epithet; *Cage Me a Peacock* is precisely what one means by 'a musical comedy'; *Fings Ain't What They Used t'Be* could only be 'a musical'. All three are excellent in their *genre*. One would not, however, like to be accused of attempting to coin some new critical usage. Often, as with the terms 'a show', 'a piece', 'a play', they are simply alternated to avoid the monotony which threatens when there are only a few terms available to describe the kind of entertainment about which one is writing.

During the past sixty years, Britain has produced few musicals to match the originality of *Oklahoma!* or *Annie Get Your Gun* or *West Side Story* – perhaps, in those six decades, only *Jesus Christ Superstar* represents any real break-through. The British public was demanding, in 1916, nothing much more adventurous than a continuation of the good old tradition established by George Edwardes at the Gaiety and Daly's; in the seventies, shows like *I and Albert, Tom Brown's Schooldays* and *Trelawny* indicate that light music composers at least believe that the public is still mainly interested in nostalgia, while in *Billy* one saw again an example of the somewhat indifferent musical 'carried' by its star – Michael Crawford doing precisely what Bobby Howes did in *Yes Madam?* and Lupino Lane in *Me and My Girl*.

But one should not fall into the error of denigrating the many enjoyable musicals which have been staged in England. If the real home of the musical in the twentieth century has been New York rather than London, our own theatres have still provided evenings of real and original pleasure in shows such as *Mr Cinders, The Dancing Years, The Boy Friend* and *Valmouth, Salad Days* and *Oliver!* Rodgers and Hart, Rodgers and Hammerstein, Cole Porter, George Gershwin, Leonard Bernstein may have broken new ground, but Ivor Novello, Noël Coward, Noel Gay, Vivian Ellis, Billy Mayerl, Jack Waller and Joseph Tunbridge, and more recently Sandy Wilson, Julian Slade, Lionel Bart and now Andrew Lloyd-Webber have given us plenty to sing about.

One's instinct, in considering the virtues of a musical, is to think first of the score – though there has been dissention about this. Noël Coward, according to his friend and secretary Cole Lesley, believed that 'the book of a musical is almost certainly the most important ingredient. The loveliest and wittiest score cannot save a weak book, nor can the most sensationally beautiful and expensive sets and costumes. All the great successful musicals have had strong books.'

Absolutely true, of course; but they have had strong scores, too, and one perhaps more readily agrees with James Agate, arguing (of *Derby Day*, in 1932) that 'a tuneful and witty score has saved a dull plot and a witless book time and time again; there is no instance of the opera that has not caught the ear being kept alive through wit in the libretto.'

So in the main we have placed the accent on composers, except where the librettists have seemed outstandingly worth attention – as was certainly the case with A. P. Herbert, the author of *Derby Day*, probably the best librettist to work in English since W. S. Gilbert. Christopher Hassall worked extremely well with Ivor Novello; at his best, Noël Coward, his own librettist, remains the only Englishman to come anywhere near matching the skill and wit deployed in New York by Cole Porter or Lorenz Hart or Ira Gershwin (though indeed there is really no contest). Two Englishmen certainly excelled in producing the books for musical comedies: but P. G. Wodehouse and Guy Bolton worked mainly on Broadway and with American composers.

If it is felt that we have been unjust to authors, then we have certainly been unjust too to impresarios – the men who so often put their money where their taste was. On the other hand none of them specialised exclusively in musicals; even C. B. Cochran and André Charlot were quite as devoted to the revue as to the musical play; other impresarios were much concerned with straight plays, too. So it seemed best to restrain ourselves from discussing them at length, in order to be able to give more space to shows which might otherwise have gone unmentioned.

We have made a few, a very few, references to musicals by non-British composers. This occurs, for instance, when a composer has worked for so long in Britain that he might be considered British by adoption, even if he was never naturalised; or when a show was so thoroughly originated in Britain and by British authors that the foreign provenance of its music seems almost irrelevant.

This book is not comprehensive in that we certainly have not mentioned every musical play produced in the West End during the sixty years covered (much less the many worthy musicals which played in the provinces and never reached London). On the other hand, we hope that every major show has been included, and we have mentioned also a number of minor, sometimes entirely forgotten shows, which for one reason or another seem interesting.

The most obvious way of dealing with the productions might have seemed to be in strictly chronological order. This proved impossible. In a number of cases, for instance, where composers had done a great deal of work over a large span of years – Coward, Novello, Ellis, Gay – it would dissipate their achievements to scatter references to their shows throughout the book. So we have dealt with them substantially in single sections, which will be found at that point in the book where, chronologically, their first or first important musical took the stage. Similarly, the musicals produced at Daly's and the Gaiety during the last years of those theatres have been dealt with in single chapters; those two theatres, so important in the British musical play tradition, seemed to deserve that much consideration. Occasionally, a production will thus be found mentioned in more than one section: *Blue Roses* is referred to both in the chapter on the Gaiety Theatre, and that on its composer, Vivian Ellis.

Undeniably, this means that the story does not read continuously, though chronological order is roughly maintained. We hope that any reader whose sense of time is staggered by the treatment we have adopted, will find it restored by a glance at the Chronological Index of productions at the end of the book, before the Index proper; here, every show mentioned in the text is listed in order of first London production, with references given to the main treatment it receives in the body of the book.

DEREK *and* JULIA PARKER
London and Foxton

Acknowledgements

In researching a subject not so far very thoroughly explored by theatre historians, much work was done at The London Library, The Westminster Public Library (which houses a large collection of theatre reference books and memoirs), and the reading room of The British Library. As always, the staffs of these institutions have been courteous and helpful and free with suggestions of sources. The National Film Institute has also been of help, and the Editor of the sixteenth edition of Pitman's *Who's Who in the Theatre*, Ian Herbert, kindly allowed us to see advance proofs. Denys Gueroult, Donald Mitchell, and Dr Stanley Sadie were also helpful. Peter Bull provided much entertaining material.

Finally, we should thank Alan Hyman, the general editor of the series of which this book is a part, for suggesting that we should work on a project which has given us a great deal of pleasure.

We are grateful to the following for permission to quote from copyright material: Oscar Asche 'Oscar Asche, His Life' (Hurst & Blackett); George Graves 'Gaieties and Gravities' (Hutchinson); C. B. Cochran 'Cock-a-doodle-doo' (J. M. Dent); Messrs. Curtis Brown, two excerpts from 'Play Parade' by Noël Coward (Heinemann); Cole Lesley 'The Life of Noël Coward (Jonathan Cape); W. Macqueen Pope 'Ivor' (W. H. Allen); Sandy Wilson 'Ivor Novello' (Michael Joseph); Vivian Ellis 'I'm on a See-Saw' (Michael Joseph); Alan Herbert 'APH' (Heinemann); Ethel Smyth 'A Final Burning of Boats' (Longmans Green); Thomas Dunhill 'Sullivan's Comic Operas' (Edward Arnold); Sandy Wilson 'I Could be Happy' (Michael Joseph); and James Agate's Estate for two excerpts from James Agate's drama reviews in 'The Contemporary Theatre' (Chapman and Hall).

We also wish to thank Keith Prowse Co Ltd. and E.M.I. for permission to quote two lyrics from 'Chu Chin Chow'; Messrs. Ascheberg, Hopwood and Crew for permission to quote two lyrics from 'The Maid of the Mountains'; Messrs. Chappell & Co. for permission to quote lyrics from 'Bitter Sweet',

'Pacific 1860', 'Big Ben', 'Bless the Bride', 'The Dancing Years' and 'The Lisbon Story', Lady Herbert for permission to quote lyrics from 'Derby Day', Faber Music Ltd. for permission to quote two lyrics from 'Paul Bunyan'; and Vivian Ellis for permission to quote lyrics from 'King of the Castle', 'Tantivy Towers' and 'Adam's Opera'.

1

Chu Chin Chow Outruns the War

'A fantastic, polyphonic, polychromatic Orientalism . . . ' – THE TIMES

Oscar Asche was extremely bored. Apart from eating – and his appetite matched his enormous frame – the one thing he enjoyed most in life was golf, and arriving in Manchester one Monday morning in the spring of 1915, during a tour he and his wife were making of the English provinces, he had been ready to spend most of his days on the links before making his way to the theatre. But that very day the Manchester rain had begun coming down in stair-rods, and by Tuesday morning it was obvious that there was to be very little chance of golf for some days.

After he had spent some days moodily surveying the downpour, his wife suggested that to pass the time he might do far worse than write the pantomime he had always said he had in mind. So he hired a typist, settled down in a corner of his hotel, dictated to her steadily each day, and by the end of the week had written half of the 'pantomime', including some lyrics and descriptions of the sets and costumes. He read the result to his old chief, Sir Frank Benson, who liked it; and three weeks later, alone in Glasgow, he wrote the second half of the play. He called it *Chu Chin Chow*, and it was to begin the revitalisation of the British musical theatre.

Not long after completing the book, Asche met, apparently by accident, the composer Frederic Norton, an ex-singer who had written the music for the successful children's play *Pinkie and the Fairies*, produced at His Majesty's in 1908 with an astonishing cast including Ellen Terry, Mrs Patrick Campbell, and several younger players including Marie Lohr and Hermione Gingold. Norton read the script of *Chu Chin Chow*, liked it, and agreed to write the music. Then came the business of trying to arrange a production.

Asche first offered the show to Robert Evett, the manager of Daly's theatre. Evett might be supposed to have a good nose for a success – he had been running Daly's since the death of the great impresario George Edwardes, and was later to present *The Maid of the Mountains* there. But he told Asche that any production of *Chu Chin Chow* would be a waste of time and money (Asche always believed that he never bothered to read it). Asche believed in his work sufficiently to take the gamble of engaging Joseph Harker to make models of the thirteen scenes in the show, and

Oscar Asche, magnificent as 'The Great Abu Hassan' in his own spectacularly successful *Chu Chin Chow*.

Percy Anderson to design the costumes, and then persuaded the manager of His Majesty's to get a small party of prospective backers together to hear the play and its music.

Having listened and looked, the company was impressed, and Henry Dana, who was managing His Majesty's for Sir Herbert Beerbohm Tree cabled the actor, then touring in America, informing him that £3000 of his money was about to be invested in a new musical. One wonders to what extent Sir Herbert was delighted? *Pinkie and the Fairies* had indeed been produced at His Majesty's, and so had a revival of Offenbach's *Orpheus* (entitled, in 1911, *Orpheus in the Underground*) – Frederic Norton had rearranged some of the music. But the theatre was not at that time particularly associated with musical comedy.

However that may be, the production of *Chu Chin Chow* went ahead. Altogether, £6000 was raised, and Asche's royalties were fixed at 6% of takings up to £1500 a week, and 10% thereafter. Since he was also producing, he asked for an additional producer's fee; the backers were not at all enthusiastic about this, and came up with what was apparently a fool-proof method of ensuring that he only received his author's royalties. If, they said, the play took in £50,000 at the box office in under twenty weeks, Asche could claim an extra 20% on all receipts over £1500 a week. Since this had never happened before in the history of the English theatre, they must have felt pretty safe.

Chu Chin Chow, having rehearsed for four weeks, opened earlier than had first been announced – Asche heard that several of his production ideas had been pirated and were to be used in a new revue, so he advanced his opening night. The press was almost unanimous in its praise. The piece, said *The Times*, was 'a fantastic, polyphonic, polychromatic Orientalism', another *Kismet*, 'everything by turns and nothing long – a series of scenes now romantic, now realistic, now Futurist or Vorticist, but always beautiful'. Indeed, it was a splendid pantomime.

Asche had based his piece on the story of *Ali Baba and the Forty Thieves*, loosely adapted from the original in *The Book of the Thousand Nights and One Night*. Kasim Baba, a rich merchant, is preparing a feast to welcome the inestimably richer Chinese merchant, Chu Chin Chow. Kasim's beautiful slave, Marjanah, is in love with his nephew Nur-al-Huda, while another of his slaves, Alcolom, is in love with his drunken meddling brother, Ali Baba, and both want their freedom in order to marry their lovers. Zahrat, a third slave, is in fact a spy placed in Kasim's house by the great Abu Hassan, a robber king, who is holding her lover hostage in order to force her to obey him.

Chu Chin Chow arrives at Kasim's house, and is revealed to be Abu Hassan in disguise. Meanwhile, Ali Baba has by accident discovered Hassan's hideaway cave, full of stolen jewels and gold, and opening of course to the cry of 'Open, Sesame!' At a slave sale, Hassan buys Zahrat and chains her up in his cave, suspicious that she has betrayed him. Ali Baba leads his brother, Kasim, to the cave where, crazed with greed, he is discovered and slaughtered. Nur and Marjanah bring the body home, and lead a blind cobbler to Kasim's house to prepare his body for burial. In return for a bribe, the cobbler attempts to lead Hassan to the house – for Hassan does not know that it was Kasim who had discovered his hoard. Meanwhile, however, Zahrat (released by Nur and the others) has duplicated on every door in the city the blue cross with which the blind man had marked the house in which he had sewn a shroud.

At a spectacular feast for the wedding of Nur and Marjanah, Zahrat persuades Hassan to hide with his forty thieves in huge oil jars, so that they can emerge from them to slaughter the guests and steal their goods. But she has also arranged that boiling oil should be poured into the jars on the unsuspecting heads of the thieves, disposing of them all – except Hassan, whom she stabs with her own hands as he advances on the company with drawn sword. A wedding procession ends the evening.

No-one could pretend that the book is either very rational or an improvement on the original tale; but it does provide ample scope for displays of *bravura* in acting, singing, and dancing, and Asche made it a magnificent show. Percy Anderson's costumes were really splendid, both for men and women: *The Times* spoke of 'audacious décolletage in both black and white, a gorgeous heap of coloured stuffs' and of 'spiral costumes, conchoidal costumes, elliptical costumes, costumes that seem to realise the very wildest dreams of our most recent artistic decadents – a really amazing wardrobe'.

Chu Chin Chow, in the true tradition of light musical theatre, opened at His Majesty's on August 31, 1916, ran for 2238 performances (a record which stood for almost half a century), and lasted longer than the Great War itself. Sir Herbert Tree, returning from America, viewed it unenthusiastically, and with the diaphanous costumes in mind, is said to have made the comment: 'I see – more navel than military'. Not a very good joke; but perhaps Sir Herbert was simply irritated by being kept out of his own theatre by a long-running musical.

The production itself seems to have aimed at reproducing even the smells of the East (a number of animals took part, including a camel, a donkey, a bullock, sheep, poultry, snakes and a horse). The human cast was headed by Asche himself as Abu Hassan, in what seems to have been a really overpowering performance, and Lily Brayton, his wife, as Zahrat – who shared with Asche an enormous enjoyment of heavy mock-Eastern accents and 'mugging'.

Ali Baba was played by Courtice Pounds, an experienced musical comedy man who had appeared with the original D'Oyly Carte Company

Courtice Pounds as Ali Baba in *Chu Chin Chow* (1916) – the part delightfully played in the later film by George Robey. Sydney Fairbrother is in the chair, and the set is striking, for its time, in realism.

at the Savoy, and was a splendid tenor as well as an accomplished actor. (In the excellent film later made of *Chu Chin Chow* – George Robey played Ali, giving perhaps his best film performance.)

There was little doubt from the start of the run that *Chu Chin Chow* was going to be a success. It easily brought £51,000 into the box office in its first seventeen weeks, and Asche went happily off to the management to claim £520 in addition to his £60 a week royalty, as his success bonus. The production, which had cost £5356.17s.9d to mount, made over £200,000 for Asche alone.

There is no doubt that his talents as a producer did much for *Chu Chin Chow*. But the other ingredients were right, too. Norton's music remains entirely delightful sixty years later. 'The Robbers' March' has become a cliché; but 'Any Time's Kissing Time' (for Alcolom and Ali Baba), 'I Love Thee So' (for Marjanah), and the lively quartet 'Mahbuba' (for Marjanah, Ali Baba, Alcolom and Kasim, supported by a chorus) still retain their freshness, while 'The Cobbler's Song' (which Frank Cochrane, doubling the roles of Kasim and the Cobbler, sang to much effect in the original production) is still regularly heard at village concerts. And Norton's originality showed in such scenes as that of the slave auction: his sequence for the slave auctioneer, 'Behold!', is not a thousand miles from Puccini either in technique or effect.

Asche's book is perhaps no more than competent, nor did his lyrics show any special talent, though he packed them with atmosphere, as in the opening number which is an introduction to the fare prepared in Kasim's kitchen:

Here be oysters stewed in honey
And conger eels cooled in snow –
Here be shellfish stuffed with olives,
And fricasseed sturgeon roe . . .

Here be lambs-tails baked in butter
And plovers' eggs from the farm –
Here be humming-birds in jelly
And lizards from Zanzibar . . .

And the comedy is sound enough. If there is no sign of real wit, there is plenty of mild good humour, as in Ali's 'When a Pullet is Plump':

When a pullet is plump, she's tender.
When she's scraggy, no teeth can rend her.
'Tis so even with a wife:
If she's fat, one blesses life –
But if she's skin and bone
She'll ever nag and moan.

Asche was an extraordinary man. He had been born at Geelong, Victoria, Australia, in 1871, the son of the proprietor of Mack's Hotel there – a man possibly of necessity so strong that he could crush a pewter pot in one hand. Oscar left Melbourne Grammar School at sixteen with an insatiable lust for adventure, and immediately set off on a six-month trip to China with a school-friend. Back home, he endured only a short spell as a store-keeper before leaving for Fiji with another friend. Then, still in his teens, he decided to go to Norway to become an actor!

The attraction of Norway was two-fold: there lived not only the great dramatist Henrik Ibsen, but the great director Bjorn Bjornson, with whom Asche studied in Christiana. It was Ibsen who gave him the rather obvious advice that since English was his native tongue, England was probably the place in which he could hope to make his fortune. And it was at the Opéra Comique in London, in 1893, that Asche made his first stage appearance. It was a brief appearance, however; soon, he was out of work and starving. He slept out on the Embankment at night, and called cabs outside theatres in the evenings to make a few coppers.

Fortunately, however, he had played a little cricket in Geelong, and this commended him to the actor-manager Sir Frank Benson, who (it was said) chose actors for his repertory company largely for their prowess on the cricket-field. Asche found himself a member of the company, playing behind the wicket and in an enormous variety of parts. He stayed with Benson's company for eight years, and in it met his wife, the actress Lily Brayton.

In 1904, the Asches joined forces with a colleague to manage the Adelphi Theatre in London, where they presented Shakespeare and a range of plays. In 1907 they went to His Majesty's, where again Shakespeare provided the staple diet, and Asche gave his Othello, said to have been one of the best interpretations of the role to be seen on the stage of that time. At the Garrick, in 1911, he played Haaj in Edward Knoblock's *Kismet* – a sort of dress rehearsal for the part he was to write for himself in *Chu Chin Chow*.

Chu Chin Chow itself made him a small fortune of £200,000 – not *so* small at the beginning of the century. He spent it all, and left only £20 in his estate when he died. No doubt much of his money went in gambling, which he loved; but a considerable amount went in mounting less successful productions – including some worthy experiments, such as his *Merry Wives of Windsor* in modern dress, in 1929. He was in many ways in advance of his time, as his productions showed. When he produced that other great success *The Maid of the Mountains* at Daly's in 1917, he physically cut away the front of the stage leaving a twelve-foot gap between actors and audience. It may have looked as though this was a device to enhance the drama of the mountain scene, and no doubt in part it was. But as Asche reveals in his autobiography, his main object was to prevent his actors and actresses from advancing right to the footlights to belt out their big numbers, and thus hopefully to make his scenes more real. In another scene, on a seashore, he achieved much the same result by spreading rough shingle on the front of the stage and making his cast appear in bare feet.

Partly because of creaking production methods, but also for other reasons, musical comedy in London was at a low ebb by the middle of the First World War. George Edwardes, whose reign at the Gaiety, the Adelphi and Daly's had provided such memorable evenings a decade or so ago, had been caught in Bad Nauheim when war broke out; repatriated on health grounds, he returned to England, but died in October 1915. By that time, revue was on the way up, having displaced music-hall and variety at the Empire, the Alhambra and the Hippodrome. Though *The Bing Boys are Here* was produced at the Alhambra, to run for almost 400 performances with George Robey, Violet Loraine and Alfred Lester, it was not a genuine musical comedy, and its score was substantially by the American composer

Nat D. Ayer – with additional numbers by Ivor Novello, Eustace Ponsonby and Philip Braham, and the book was written by the British musical comedy star George Grossmith, in collaboration with Fred Thompson.

Chu Chin Chow held the centre-stage firmly. It became a positive mania. One Lancashire family booked the same set of eight stalls on the first Tuesday of every month for the entire run. Men at the front took their girl-friends, every time they came on leave, and carried back with them fragile shellac recordings to play on wind-up gramophones in the trenches. There were some touching incidents; on the last night of the show, in 1921, an elderly lady was seen sitting in the stalls with a vacant seat next to her, on which was a school cap. She explained to Asche afterwards that she had heard *Chu Chin Chow* every year on the anniversary of the evening on which she had taken her son to His Majesty's on his last leave before being killed on the Somme. The cap was his.

Throughout the war, performances were occasionally interrupted by air raids. The flutter of a handkerchief from the prompt corner would warn the cast to stop playing, and an announcement would be made; the safety curtain would be lowered, and the audience would file from its seats into the passages surrounding the stalls, beneath the pavements of the Haymarket. Meanwhile, the cast would generally take to the roof to watch the excitement.

There were sometimes other forms of excitement, usually provided by some of the many animals in the cast. They all seemed to behave decorously on-stage; off-stage there were incidents, as when the man in charge of the camel took his eye off that beast for a moment, when it fell through a pavement-light and was killed. Its guardian warned Mr Asche not to eat out in Soho for an evening or two: he had sold the body to an eager restaurant owner. Then there was Sarah, the donkey, who would occasionally get bored with merely carrying Courtice Pounds about the stage, would escape through the stage door, and cantering up to Piccadilly Circus reduce the traffic there to chaos before making happily for Vine Street Police Station, where she was well known, and there wait to be collected and taken back to the theatre.

Armistice night was naturally a great occasion. Asche devised a special scene: after the closing of the show proper, girls in the national dress of each Allied country entered to the relevant national anthem, followed by Lily Brayton as Brittania, accompanied by more girls representing the countries of the British Empire. To the strains of 'Rule, Brittania!' she released a white dove, 'which fluttered around the auditorium, returned to the stage and rested on the draperies of France. This unrehearsed happy effect created the wildest of enthusiasm.' Oscar Asche then came on dressed as John Bull, and delivered a patriotic oration. The pageant was so popular that it was kept in for six months.

The last night was as enthusiastic as the first. The money taken was a box-office record (£503 at specially raised prices). Not surprisingly, Asche was tempted to try to repeat the formula in *Cairo*, for which once more he wrote both book and lyrics, and for which Percy Fletcher composed the music. At first, the show was called *Mecca*, but the Lord Chamberlain insisted that the title was one which might give offence to British Jewry. Whereupon Mr Asche sent him several cuttings from the Press advertising such goods as the Mecca Pills for Piles; but he would not change his mind.

Cairo, produced in four weeks, opened at His Majesty's three months after the closure of *Chu Chin Chow* – on October 15, 1921. It was extremely elaborate – to an extent which gave some trouble, for only the day before the opening it was discovered that two giant bronze gates, which drew back to disclose one scene, crossed the line of the safety curtain by half an inch, and twelve hours' work had to be done to rebuild the set. *Cairo* was only a moderate success – though it ran for 267 performances and made a profit of £12,000 (so its failure was relative!) The audience was probably drawn by Asche's reliance, once more, on diaphanous costumes, and by the notoriety of one particular scene: an orgy held by the villain in an old, ruined Egyptian palace where, Asche claimed, 'Cleopatra and her countless lovers, ages ago, did carouse, disport and sin.' One member of the first-night audience breathily described the scene:

> A line of flickering, flaming braziers competed with the moonlight which drenched the scene. All was silence. Then a perfect tidal wave of humanity, half-naked, howling, singing, laughing and shouting, broke over the stage. The brass blared, cymbals crashed, and drums thundered and throbbed as that mob went seemingly crazy. Every thing was bizarre, fantastic, utterly uninhibited. Women who seemed almost nude were lifted aloft on the shoulders of men, to be dragged down and embraced in abandoned attitudes by other men. Girls like furies with flowing hair of green, red and all other hues threw themselves on the villain, who sat enthroned like a prince, smothered him with lascivious gestures, and fought for his favour. It was wildly virile, a very whirlpool of colour, noise and ceaseless movement. When the orgy was at its height, the curtain fell so suddenly that it took the audience by surprise. Then almost immediately it rose again on a picture which left them breathless. The noise, the movement and the music had gone. There was silence. The crowd of revellers, worn out with excesses, were strewn about in heaps everywhere, utterly exhausted, a human débris, massed, conglomerate, their white limbs gleaming in the moonlight and the torches' glow. The festival of Saturn in ancient Rome could not have been more ravishing to the eye.

But to return to 1916, the year of the birth of *Chu Chin Chow*: competition from other home-produced shows was not very considerable. W. H. Berry, the comedian, was a big draw at the Adelphi in *High Jinks* – but again, the book was adapted from the French, and the music was by Rudolph Friml. In September an English musical did open at the Comedy: *This and That*, composed by James W. Tate for his wife Clarice Mayne. They were a somewhat strange couple, usually billed at variety theatres as 'Clarice Mayne and "That" ' – 'That' being her husband. Their adventure into musical comedy was not a great success, though the book was by an experienced author, Harry Grattan, mainly known then for his revue sketches but later the author of one of the first radio comedy series, *Erb and Emma*. It was mainly an excuse for Miss Mayne to appear in a large number of beautiful dresses, sing a series of songs, and do a few of her celebrated impersonations.

My Lady Frayle, which opened at the Shaftesbury in March 1916, had come off by the time *Chu Chin Chow* opened: one of its stars, Courtice Pounds, went into the latter show. It was not entirely unamusing, however, concerning a middle-aged lady who invoked the Devil to help her steal a young man away from his girl-friend. An American tenant of Lady Frayle's house, one Lucifer D. Nation, changed the elderly lady into his young niece, with whom of course the young man fell instantly in love. What happened to his soul (Mr Nation's price for the deal) was never revealed, but the plot gave plenty of opportunity to Mr Pounds, who stole most of the notices for his performance as a Canon of Doncaster. Cecil Humphreys played Lucifer with considerable flair.

But there was nothing much to endear the piece to a popular audience. Arthur Wimperis and Max Pemberton had apparently not made up their minds quite what style to assume in the book and the music, though by the experienced Howard Talbot and Herman Finck, did not take.

Talbot , whose real name was Howard Munkittrick, had been born in New York, though as he came to England almost before he could walk, he is generally regarded as English. He was educated (as a medical student) at King's College, London, but then at the Royal College of Music under Hubert Parry. There was little question of his ever practising medicine, even when his marriage to a young English girl made a stable career desirable. He had something of a *succés d'estime* with his early comic opera *Wapping Old Stairs*, performed in 1894, *Monte Carlo* (1896) and *A Chinese Honeymoon* (1899), which ran for over 1000 performances, a record for a musical play at that time. He was to conduct at Daly's, the Adelphi and the Prince of Wales, and was to write *The Arcadians* (with Lionel Monckton, in 1909) and *My Nieces* (1921) before his death in 1928. During his last illness, his late work *All Hail Our King*, a march, was played on the radio; he was too ill to hear it.

Herman Finck, his collaborator on *My Lady Frayle*, was a product of the Guildhall School of Music, and had begun playing in a theatre orchestra at the age of fourteen. He was musical director of the Palace Theatre for twenty years, and had conducted in many other theatres. His compositions had included much incidental music, and some of his separate numbers – 'In the Shadows', for instance – had a success in their time. But his long list of shows contains no really memorable titles. *My Lady Frayle* itself ran for only 130 performances – partly because the music lacked superficial attractiveness. Some critics indeed complained that it was 'too operatic'.

That was a complaint also made of Sydney Jones' music for *The Happy Day*, produced at Daly's in 1916; that, and the infinitely more successful *The Maid of the Mountains*, will be considered in the following chapter. In the meantime, *The Bing Boys are Here* (which had opened in April 1916) was followed in February 1917 by *The Bing Girls are There*, which opened at the Alhambra, again with music by Nat D. Ayer and words by Grossmith and Fred Thompson. Perhaps since at the least the books of these shows were English, one might glance at the thin thread of narrative which strung one of them together; all three were billed as 'a revue'.

In *The Bing Girls are There*, two girls, Emerald and Amethyst, left their country home at Lesser Binghampton for Blackpool and London, where they encountered Oswald Marigold, a young man who, like Madame Husson's May King, had won a prize for good behaviour, but was now living a life of wild dissipation, aided by Cissie and Kissie, the two bad girls of Lesser Binghampton. The sketches this vestigial plot encouraged can be imagined, and were played to the hilt by Violet Loraine and Joseph Coyne, on the romantic side (Coyne had been the leading man in *The Merry Widow*: crowds would gather to see him eating ice-cream at Lyons' Corner House at St Giles' Circus), and by Wilkie Bard, in drag, as Emerald. Lorna and Toots Pounds appeared as the bad sisters.

In August 1917, to the Prince of Wales, came *Carminetta*, based on the adventures of the alleged daughter of Carmen and Don José, with music by Herman Finck, Emile Lassaily and Herman Darewski. Lassaily is a shadowy figure: Darewski a rather extraordinary one. He was a Russian, born at Minsk in 1883, who was educated in London and then in Vienna, and returned to England overflowing with music – none of it, it must be admitted, outstanding. One or two numbers had a success, however: notably 'Au Revoir, My Little Hyacinth', which he wrote for Ellaline Terriss to sing in *The Beauty of Bath* (1906). He subsequently turned out an enormous number of songs for revues and musical plays.

Practice was evidently what he needed, for by the time war broke out he had a certain facility which showed itself in some celebrated novelty songs, including the renowned 'Sister Susie's Sewing Shirts for Soldiers' and its lesser-known sequels 'Mother's Sitting Knitting Little Mittens for the Navy' and 'Which Switch is the Switch, Miss, for Ipswich?'. 'I Used to Sigh for the Silv'ry Moon', 'If You Could Care for Me', and 'Whispering' show a lyrical gift which anyone might envy, but which was somehow seldom at its best in his musicals, and certainly found little release in *Carminetta* – though he did write the hit song for that show, with which Alice

Delysia delighted audiences. With his considerable talent for unwieldy titles, it was determinedly called 'Oh, Bless You, Damn You, Clicquot, You Make the World Go Round'. The play ran for 260 performances.

In December 1917, at the Palace, Lily Elsie, the star of *The Merry Widow*, returned to the musical stage after a long interval. After *The Count of Luxembourg* at Daly's in 1911, she had retired from the stage to marry, and it was not until the production of *Pamela* that she was heard again in musical comedy. *Pamela* had a rather difficult birth: Gerald du Maurier had been interested in it, but had been too ill to carry his interest through, and it was another matinée idol, Owen Nares (whose acting career had in fact been rather more substantial, though certainly no less successful, than du Maurier's) took the leading role. G. P. Huntley, an experienced and popular comedian from Daly's and elsewhere, also played.

The plot was a nothing: Miss Elsie was a beautiful rich girl to whom a group of admirers paid court. The piece was moderately well received by the critics ('the scenery and dresses are all that could be expected or desired; the music is light and pretty, and the company strong all through') and it ran for 172 performances despite being regularly interrupted by air raids, which even slightly damaged the theatre. The book of *Pamela* was by Arthur Wimperis, who had written lyrics for *The Arcadians* and *My Lady Frayle*, and the music was by Frederic Norton: none of it has survived.

The best-remembered, and probably the best show of 1917 was *The Boy*, staged at the Adelphi in September, which ran for 801 performances. This was an adaptation by Fred Thompson of Arthur Pinero's farce *The Magistrate*, with music by Lionel Monckton and Howard Talbot. The music was excellent, but there is no doubt too that Pinero's text contributed a great deal to the success of the evening (the play is one of his best, as a more recent straight revival for the late Alistair Sim showed). It was heavily, but very skilfully cut by Thompson, and writers of musical comedies who insist that the book of a musical is as important as the music are certainly supported by the success of *The Boy*, for none of the numbers in it have lasted.

The production was well cast: W. H. Berry, as Valentine Meebles, spoke his songs rather in the manner re-invented in our own time by Rex Harrison for *My Fair Lady*. Maisie Gay, Nellie Taylor, Peter Gawthorne and Billie Carlton appeared, together with C. M. Lowne, a straight actor and most accomplished light comedian. But it was Berry's show: with *High Jinks* and now *The Boy*, he established himself as a comedian who could,

Lily Elsie looking enchanting in *Pamela* (1917). She had made a sensation as Sonia in *The Merry Widow* in 1907; in *Pamela* she played a rich girl surrounded by admirers. And no wonder.

A playbill for *The Boy*, the Monckton & Talbot musical version of Pinero's The Magistrate (1917).

W. H. Berry as the magistrate who spent some time disguised as a waiter in *The Boy*: he peels off his false moustache at the end of the episode.

most unusually, be the main attraction in a musical – a place he usurped from the leading lady. *The Boy* became extremely fashionable – in Dornford Yates' Berry books the Pleydells are always clamouring to re-visit it.

There is a sense in which all these musicals, even *Chu Chin Chow*, were somewhat unexpected: none of them played at either of the two theatres particularly celebrated as the home of musical comedy – Daly's and the Gaiety. But these two theatres demand chapters of their own.

2

The Last Years of the Gaiety

'You're all lovely!' – A LADY IN THE GALLERY

It was George Edwardes who had made the Gaiety Theatre, in the Strand, famous as a home of musical comedy during the closing years of the nineteenth century and the first decade of the twentieth. He had a flair for picking happy, tuneful and entertaining shows and casting them with talented stars and beautiful girls; he invented what London thought of as 'the Gaiety show'; and with his death an era ended.

The Gaiety was substantially left in the hands of George Dance, who had started life as the writer of not very good songs for various music-hall celebrities, and turned to writing musical comedies (the best, *A Chinese Honeymoon*, had a run of over 1000 performances just after the turn of the century). After a spell managing a number of touring companies which took successes from the Gaiety and Daly's out to provincial theatres all over England, he had taken up residence in the Strand. (He was later to buy a knighthood by presenting Lilian Baylis with £30,000 to save the Old Vic.)

Dance was approached early in 1915 by a new theatrical partnership – George Grossmith, the son of a famous Gilbert and Sullivan star, and Edward Laurillard. Grossmith was a well-known musical comedy performer who had played at the Gaiety many times. His partner, Laurillard, had been born in Rotterdam and educated in Paris. In his twenties, he had gone into theatrical production in London, and at one time was responsible for running over twenty-five 'cinema-theatres'. With Grossmith he was to present sixteen musicals in London before their partnership was dissolved in 1921. Dance knew the ebullient Grossmith well; and he was impressed by the apparent business acumen of Laurillard, though the latter's haphazard command of English made it extremely difficult to know just what he was proposing – not always a disadvantage during financial negotiations.

The partners came to the Gaiety with one success already on record: *Potash and Perlmutter*, a comedy which they had presented at the Queen's in April 1914, and which had immediately captured an audience and run for 664 performances. They proposed to Dance that he should allow them to bring to the Gaiety a musical which they had presented in New York at

Christmas. It had got good notices there, many of them concentrating on one young Englishman of twenty-four, to whom Grossmith and Laurillard had given a chance. Leslie Henson was to become, during the next thirty years, one of the best known and most popular stars of musical comedy in England.

Henson had started life as a businessman, though for a while he attended a drama school. Soon, theatre got its claws into him, and he started appearing in concert party, and then was engaged by Dance to appear in the touring company of *The Quaker Girl*. That was in 1912; and after a single London engagement, he had been sent to New York with *Tonight's The Night*. Fortunately for him, the illness of a colleague enabled him to take over a leading role; he made a success in it – especially in a song of his own, 'Murders' – and Grossmith and Laurillard had no hesitation in inviting him to appear in the London production.

The music of *Tonight's The Night* was by Paul Rubens, the composer of a number of successes (though, ironically, not of the hit number of that particular show, 'They Didn't Believe Me', which was one of two songs interpolated into the score and written by a young American, Jerome Kern). The play itself was adapted from a popular farce, *Pink Dominoes*, by James Albery, first seen in London in 1877, and already twice revived in its original form.

In the London production, Grossmith himself appeared, with Madge Saunders as his beautiful leading lady. She was so beautiful indeed that the Sultan of Zanzibar, visiting the Gaiety one evening, fell deeply in love with her, and informed the management that he wished to buy her. He was politely discouraged, and she later married Leslie Henson. Grossmith had an enormous personal success in 'They Didn't Believe Me', and also appropriated to himself the comic song which Henson had sung with such *élan* in New York. 'Murders' was a number in which the singer, in impeccable evening dress and an advanced state of inebriation, confessed to a large number of murders he had committed. Grossmith seems to have done it exceptionally well; and Henson does not seem to have minded too much, for he himself was well liked by both critics and public, and *Tonight's The Night* set him forth on his successful career. It ran for 460 performances, and was very popular with the young men who, on leave from the front, wanted above all an entertainment which, like *Chu Chin Chow*, would take them out of themselves.

The war came to the Gaiety in a more immediate way than simply the presence of khaki uniforms in the stalls. A bomb falling outside the Lyceum Theatre, across the road, was followed by another which wrecked a pub nearby, killing both an electrician who had slipped out of the Gaiety for a pint, and 'Nelson', the one-eyed messenger-boy who also worked at the theatre. A third bomb, falling fifty yards down the road, injured the

Gaiety's call-boy.

But that is by the way: the London theatre has never been very intimidated by violence, and *Tonight's The Night* played on through those explosions and several more to come. Perhaps Grossmith and Laurillard were indeed going to recapture the great days of the Gaiety? It seemed so. When *Tonight's The Night* ended its run, it was replaced by *Theodore & Co.*, for which Jerome Kern wrote some of the music, and the rest was by the young Ivor Novello. Leslie Henson was, this time, right at the top of the bill, and in Novello's song 'My Friend John' established himself thoroughly with a London audience that was to laugh with him and support him for the rest of his life. He sang it every night for over 500 performances.

But by the end of the run, the Gaiety had changed managements: it had been taken over by Alfred Butt, who at that time was also running the Empire, the Palace, the Victoria Palace, the Globe and the Queen's. On the face of it, this need not necessarily have been a bad thing. Butt (to be knighted in 1929) was an extremely experienced manager, who had left his accounting desk at Harrod's to become secretary at the Shaftesbury Theatre, then assistant manager, then manager, and eventually managing director. It was as managing director that he took control of the Gaiety – and when one looks at his subsequent career, which included the mounting of such successful American shows as *Rose Marie*, *The New Moon*, *The Desert Song*, *Show Boat* and *Funny Face*, one wonders that he was not able to maintain the impetus which Grossmith and Laurillard had given to an almost reborn Gaiety.

Well, he was not; and one of the reasons was, no doubt, that those two men did not choose to work for him. They took their talents, and what amounted to a private repertory company, to the Prince of Wales and the Shaftesbury, and then in 1919 to the Winter Garden, in Drury Lane. The Gaiety was the poorer without them.

Butt's first show at the Gaiety was *The Beauty Spot*, adapted from the French by Arthur Anderson, and with a score by James W. Tate. Tom Walls, in ten years' time to be one of an extraordinary team of *farceurs* at the Aldwych, was in the cast, with Régine Flory as the leading lady. The story was about an elderly gentleman who claimed to have written *the* definitive work about Baluchistan when, as became clearer and clearer, he had never been there – and was soon being blackmailed on that account.

It was not inordinately successful, but Maisie Gay, a George Edwardes girl who had appeared in *A Waltz Dream*, *Our Miss Gibbs* and *The Quaker Girl*, made a great effect in a yodelling duet and Mlle Flory danced a somewhat sensational 'hashish dance' with Jan Oyra, a Russian who had been injured during service in the Russian Army, and had a silver plate set in his skull which, if anyone touched it, rendered him instantly unconscious – a hazard of which the cast was soon sensible.

The Beauty Spot ran for 152 performances, and then Butt staged a musical which had been offered to him together with the enormously successful *The Lilac Domino* by an illiterate Russian with a nose for a successful show – Joseph Leonard Sacks. Sacks had gone to South Africa when he was nine, and by the time he was nineteen was presenting shows there, despite the fact that he could neither read nor write. In 1918, he approached Butt having acquired the rights of Cuvillier's enchanting operetta, and of *Going Up*, with a book by James Montgomery and Otto Harbach, and music by Louis Hirsch, *Going Up* opened at the Gaiety on May 22, 1918.

It was an American show, and we must not linger to consider it in detail: but the cast was thoroughly English – Evelyn Laye, who had had her first real chance on the West End stage when she had taken over a principal role in *The Beauty Spot*, was now cast in a larger part, and appeared with that most popular of musical comedy heroes, Joseph Coyne, who played the author of a book on aviation who was transformed into the popular flying idol of a seaside resort: this was probably the first time that an aeroplane played a substantial part in a musical comedy.

Coyne appeared opposite that great favourite Ruby Miller, who had started life as a Shakespearean actress, but was better-known for her more glamorous roles in musical comedy. It was from her slipper that a besotted admirer once actually drank a champagne toast, apologising next morning by sending her two dozen new pairs. Later, an even more eccentric admirer filled her bedroom with gardenia petals, on which she fell asleep to the sounds of a gypsy orchestra he had installed in the next room. Well, her beauty no doubt merited such attentions, and she and Mr Coyne certainly drew the crowds to *Going Up*, where they not only enthused over them, but over Miss Laye, and in particular over 'The Tickle Toe', a new dance which had, the amazed public was informed, 'thirteen separate movements'!

Going Up came off in July 1919, and *The Kiss Call* followed it – a musical written by Fred Thompson, with music by Ivan Caryll (a Belgian whose real name was Tilkins, and who had both conducted at the Gaiety and written musical comedies which were staged there). Its star was G. P. Huntley, a marvellous comedian who though only middle-aged was unfortunately right at the end of his career and drinking heavily. The show ran, or in Mr Huntley's case staggered, for 176 performances, with a good supporting cast in which were Austin Melford, Evelyn Laye, Stanley Lupino and Binnie Hale.

Then came a revival of *The Shop Girl*, followed by a production of Maeterlinck's *The Betrothal*, with Bobby Andrews and Gladys Cooper. Not strictly a musical, it contained nevertheless a substantial amount of music by C. Armstrong Gibbs, who devised themes to introduce each character as he stepped onto the stage (therefore, alas, too often drowned by welcoming applause), and whose ballet music, based on old themes such as 'Little Bo-Peep' and 'The Three Jolly Postboys', was much admired.

The Betrothal had a fairly good run of 111 performances; but this was not good enough for the Gaiety. What was to follow? Someone had the idea of reviving burlesque – a form which had been successful in the theatre of the 1850s. But *Faust-on-Toast*, with a book written in rhyming couplets by Firth Shephard, was not to be the answer.

The author converted the story of Faust into modern terms, with Marguerite as a film-star, Valentine as her agent, and with Jack Buchanan as the Devil himself. George Grossmith, now happily running the Winter Garden, returned as producer, and brought in Willie Warde, ballet-master at the old Gaiety, to stage the dances. Another piece of insurance was the introduction of a *scena* which contained reprises of some of the numbers made famous at the Gaiety in former years – 'Linger Longer, Lucy', 'The Bogey Man', and others, and a special performance of the famous *pas de quatre* which had been the sensation of *Faust-up-to-Date* in 1888, and which Ward remembered perfectly.

The last item was the only one in the show which pleased a noisy and dissatisfied audience on the first night (May 12, 1921). Despite the excellent cast (Maisie Gay was also one of the players), the burlesque was heavy and unamusing – the rhymed couplets fell like lead into the stalls, and prevented the comedians from ad-libbing, which was of the essence in burlesque. The show lost the management over £40,000.

The next Gaiety musical was remarkable only for the reason that it starred Stanley Lupino. *His Girl* had been written by Austin Hurgon and F. W. Thomas, and had music by Ernest Longstaffe and Max Darewski (Darewski well known, Longstaffe almost completely unknown, though much later to become a well-known figure in radio). *His Girl* was moderately amusing, with clever lyrics by Claude E. Burton. But its main attraction was Lupino, a member of a famous theatrical family, who had formerly been best known in pantomime. *His Girl* gave him his first major role in musical comedy in the West End as an unpolished diamond with amorous proclivities, and he made the best of it, amusing himself and the audience at the expense of a peculiarly precocious child actress, Vesta Sylva, who was so set on making her own mark that no amount of sending-up by Lupino offended her.

Meanwhile, there had been an upset at George Edwardes' other great theatre, Daly's. The theatre had been sold, and Robert Evett, who had worked with Edwardes for a decade, and had been managing Daly's since the Guv'nor's death, could not get on with its new owner, James White. He left Daly's for the Gaiety, where he made a determined effort to bring back the good old days – and got off to a remarkably good start by presenting Oscar Straus' *The Last Waltz*, in a production by Charles Hawtrey, and with José Collins as its star.

Miss Collins had a triumph on the first night in a piece which had all the charm of the best Viennese light operettas, and which had been elegantly and wittily translated into English by Reginald Arkell and Evett himself. *The Last Waltz* opened on December 7, 1922, and with the added publicity of being the first West End show to be broadcast from a theatre, it ran for 280 performances. Meanwhile, Evett was planning a presentation of *Catherine*, a piece about the Empress of Russia, which Arkell had seen in Vienna and thought a likely vehicle for Miss Collins.

Noël Coward was approached to write the English book of *Catherine*, but declined, so Arkell did it himself – and wrote the lyrics as well, which provided a taxing exercise, since the music was all well known to his audiences, being entirely abstracted from the works of Tchaikovsky. Bleeding hunks of *Casse Noisette*, the *Pathétique*, and other works accompanied the cast as they stalked through the piece in splendid Russian costumes, looking, evidently, quite magnificent; one scene especially impressed audiences – the wedding of Catherine and Czar Peter, in which Miss Collins wore an immense wedding dress of silver, and the couple walked to their thrones to the music of the *1812 Overture*!

'Queer history but good entertainment', said *The Times*, and audiences agreed; the piece ran for six months, until March 1924, and was one of José Collins' greatest triumphs – even when, as happened one night, a lift which was carrying her to stage level stuck, and she remained for some time with her legs on one side of a flat and her head on another, waving and apologising to the house the while.

She remained at the Gaiety for the next production: *Our Nell*, a musical about Nell Gwyn, with a book by Arkell and Louis N. Parker, and music by Harold Fraser-Simson and Ivor Novello. The play was metamorphosed from one entitled *Our Peg*, in which Miss Collins had appeared at Daly's in 1920, playing the part of another famous actress, Peg Woffington. Now, Peg became Nell, and her romance with Charles II was the pivot of the plot.

Our Nell pulled out all the stops: apart from Nell Gwyn's vivacity and humour (in Miss Collins' able and professional hands), it tugged away at the audience's heartstrings when she and the King were parted only to be – of course – reunited at the climax of the play, when a patriotic outburst heralded the foundation by His Majesty of the Chelsea Hospital! Arthur Wontner, looking magnificent but a bit glum, played Charles, and the young Miles Malleson was also in the cast.

The authors' wit seems to have been fairly vestigial: a fair sample of the humour was Rochester's reply when Charles gravely remarked 'We are not unmindful that a king is the father of his people.' 'Of many of them, sire', replied the courtier. But then, audiences are often too easily pleased, and at least one critic found the piece dated and its visual glories over-praised. James Agate, in *The Sunday Times*, wrote of one scene that it was played in:

> the most monstrously garish "set" that the paint brush of man has ever perpetrated. It seared the eyeballs, and for a while I literally could only bear to look at the stage for a second or so at a time, and thus gradually grow to a state of insensibility. As with some of the setting, so with most of the costumes. It may be that Mr Lovat Frazer and Mr Nigel Playfair have spoiled our taste. But take the gowns worn by Nell. They were – I speak under correction – of no discernible period, and just about as unbeautiful as the mind of Hanover Square, 1924, could devise. A fortune had doubtless been spent upon them, but not a groat's worth of taste. Still, georgette in the dressmaker's mind covers a multitude of indiscretions.

Certainly far more trouble is taken in the seventies in the dressing of period plays than it was in the twenties – even in the most serious of classical revivals, designers of that time were liable to take considerable liberties. But Mr Agate was in a minority: on the first night of *Our Nell* there were innumerable curtain calls, until eventually Miss Collins came to the front of the stage smothered in flowers, and said that while her heart was too full for words, she could still sing; the band struck up one of the songs from the show; and a chorus was repeated. Then everybody went home.

Our Nell, which ran until 1925, was the last of the short run of pieces which Evett produced at the Gaiety with José Collins as star. And now, rumbling down upon the Gaiety with all his magisterial charm, came Oscar Asche, to present *The Good Old Days*, a piece which he had written in pantomime blank verse. It was a somewhat odd play, which had little plot, and seemed in the main to be a simple presentation of a number of Dickensian characters meeting at an inn. Percy Fletcher, who had been musical director at several London theatres, had written the score of *Cairo*, and now provided some rather good music for *The Good Old Days*, including a fine first-act septet for some 'college bloods' and huntsmen, and an impressive unaccompanied chorus in Act II. But it was not enough – nor were Asche's special effects.

With his usual taste for a lively stage picture, he imported a certain amount of flora and fauna, including hounds, chickens and horses. In order to give the horses' hoofs something approaching a hard high road on which to clatter, he covered the stage with paving-stones, all thoroughly cemented down. *The Good Old Days* ran for only thirty-seven performances, and the Gaiety management found themselves at the end of it with an area of closely-paved stage on which it was necessary to spend a considerable amount of money before the boards reappeared.

The Gaiety was now badly in need of a success. There was an attempt to revive the old 'Girl' *genre* with *The Girl from Cook's*, which seems to have had its origin in an old Gaiety number, 'Follow the Girl from Cook's'. The music was by Jean Gilbert and Raymond Hubbell (the latter had written *The Man from Cook's*, in 1912). W. H. Berry, 'lustily facetious', as one critic put it, led the cast, with Edmund Gwenn, Ernest Thesiger, Eve Sternroyd (in the title role) and 'a score of young women flinging their regimental legs in various directions and rolling their eyes charmingly', as the critic of *The Times* roguishly reported. Nevertheless, the show survived for only thirty-eight performances, then giving way to *Peter Pan* at Christmas.

The Gaiety was dark, after *Peter Pan*'s short seasonal run, until June of 1928, when Louis N. Parker's *Marjolaine* was presented. The score was by Hugo Felix, a Doctor of Science of Vienna University whose main success had been *Les Merveilleuses*, in 1905. *Marjolaine* was a highly sentimental piece concerning three pairs of lovers, one young and gallant, one mature and long separated, one poor and deserving. The show also contained a chorus of muffin-men, a Punch and Judy show, a cat and a parrot; Lilian Davis took the lead, and Oscar Asche, no doubt warmly approving of the presence of the livestock, had a success as a much-married man and father who had ceased to love. At least he – and everyone else – enjoyed the first night. 'You're all lovely!' shouted one lady from the gallery as the cast took their bow. But *Marjolaine* nevertheless only ran for about four months, after which the Duncan Sisters, an American couple, presented *Topsy and Eva*, based on *Uncle Tom's Cabin*; this was a disaster from its first night (October 4, 1928), and was not even saved by Gracie Fields, who generously joined the cast in an attempt to rescue the Duncans.

On March 20, 1929, came *Love Lies*, with a book by Stanley Lupino and Arthur Rigby, and music by Hal Brody, an American. In this show Lupino started his partnership with Laddie Cliff, a comedian with considerable music-hall experience both in England and America, who had appeared in *The Bing Boys are Here* and other minor successes. But in *Love Lies* more attention was on Cyril Richard and Madge Elliott, whose dancing was a particular draw.

The show had a goodish run of 347 performances before giving way to *Darling, I Love You*, in which George Clarke, who like Laddie Cliff had had much music-hall experience, enlivened the plot, (about a lady who regularly swooned into the arms of attractive young men, and declined to budge until they whispered to her the phrase which was the show's title), by some splendid comic setpieces – an illustrated lecture on beards, and a number in which he danced, with a butler and a private secretary, a gavotte which gradually turned into a kicking match. The score was by H. B. Hedley and Harry Acres.

Stanley Lupino and Laddie Cliff teamed up to present *The Love Race*, which Lupino wrote, and which was a lively and inventive evening's entertainment in which Cyril Richard sang, charmingly, some of the numbers of Jack Clarke, whose score was on the whole rather pleasant, including certainly one tuneful waltz duet for Lupino and Drusilla Wills.

Madge Elliott in *The Love Race* (1930). In London she played in a swirl of musical comedies during the 1920s and 1930s, and later in revue.

Frederic Conyngham was particularly mentioned by several critics as an enjoyable dancer, and they also admired Madge Elliott as a heroine 'in the old tradition of cherry blossom and laburnam'. *The Love Race* ran for 237 performances.

But now come two failures: *Blue Roses* opened on January 25, 1931, written by Desmond Carter and Caswell Garth, and with music by Vivian Ellis – of whom much more in a later chapter. The score included 'I Saw the Moon Through a Window', a duet for Vera Bryer and Roy Royston, which was thoroughly enjoyed on the first night, as was the dance in which Jean Colin led the chorus on a darkened stage with little lamps on their shoes. But the show failed to take – and so did *The Millionaire Kid*, which followed it on May 20, despite the grace and vivacity of the small chorus and the effectiveness of the knockabout humour of Lupino and Cliff. The play (by Noel Scott) was set in Devonshire – somewhat surprisingly, considering the title – and the score was by Billy Mayerl (who, again, is dealt with at length later). His 'Thank You Most Sincerely', sung and danced by Madge Elliott and Cyril Richard, was perhaps the one really good song in the show.

Hold My Hand, which was produced in December 1931, had a weak book and weaker music (by Noel Gay), but the general speed and showmanship of the cast saved it for 212 performances – Stanley Lupino appeared again, as a millionaire who believed his ward to be a small child when she was in fact the fully-developed Miss Jessie Matthews. Sonnie Hale and Lupino (as a cocky mixture of self-assurance and impudence) contributed to what was a mild success.

Though it was unsuccessful, *Ballerina*, which opened at the Gaiety on October 10, 1933, remains one of the most interesting entertainments of the last decade of the theatre's life. It was 'something of a play, something of a ballet, and rather more of a musical comedy', *The Times* suggested. It told the story of a dancer's life, with the heartache and the success which attended her career. The book was by Rodney Ackland, a playwright whose *Strange Orchestra* had attracted a great deal of attention when it was produced at the St Martin's the year before. His dialogue was extremely good, though at its strongest during the earlier part of the evening, when in a series of highly effective short scenes he dealt with the dancer's early struggles.

The trouble seems to have been that the rather scrappy form of the piece militated against its success: the format couldn't cope with the dramatic content. Still, Wendy Toye (later to become a highly witty and accomplished director of operetta and musical comedy) made a success as the young dancer; Lewis Casson was effective as the impresario who died of 'gadding about in her train', as one critic unsympathetically put it; and Lydia Kyasht and Anton Dolin, two distinguished dancers, made effective 'guest appearances'. The music was by Henry Sullivan.

Interestingly enough, the next artistes to appear on the Gaiety stage were again professional dancers – the Ballet Jooss, which had been founded three years previously by Kurt Jooss. Among the ballets presented during this London season was the famous *Green Table*, a classic justly celebrated in the history of choreography.

Sporting Love, composed by Billy Mayerl to a book by Stanley Lupino and Arthur Rigby, opened on April 1, 1934. Lupino regarded most plots as rather boring attributes of musical comedy, and in this case more or less ignored the story, concentrating on a series of scenes through which three sets of lovers romped in pursuit of a fortune, adventuring with a horse which they hoped would win the Derby. Lupino was once more teamed with Laddie Cliff, and the pair of them would spend five or ten minutes elaborating a single joke, to the great delight of the audience. The show ran for over 300 performances, which was a good run for the Gaiety in its last years.

The next show, *Jack o' Diamonds*, which opened on February 25, 1935, only lasted for just over 100 performances: it was a variation, and not so much of a variation at that, on the Cinderella story, with Greta Fayne, an attractive young dancer, as the Cinderella-figure slighted by her snobbish mother and fortune-hunting sister. The entire show took place in the jade-green and silver hall of an Ascot house, which made an elegant setting for a procession of beautiful girls wearing a number of attractive gowns. The score by Noel Gay was not especially good, though there were one or two lively numbers, including a South American dance performed with great verve by Zelina O'Neal and Dino Galvani, later a member of the cast of the most famous radio show ever, ITMA.

An American show, *Gay Deceivers*, was brought in on May 23, 1935, providing a pleasant enough evening; it gave way in October to *Seeing Stars*, a loosely-constructed musical presented by Firth Shephard, whose first memory of the Gaiety was being booed as part-author of *Faust-on-Toast*.The score was by Martin Broones, the American co-composer of *Gay Deceivers*. Leslie Henson was the star – twenty-one years after his first Gaiety appearance in *Tonight's The Night*. Debroy Somers, a well-known band-leader who was to be musical director at the Gaiety until its closure, conducted. A considerable attraction was Florence Desmond, who impersonated a large selection of popular film-stars; she was, indeed, the *raison d'être* of the show. Soon after she left the cast the piece closed, and on July 9, 1936, came *Swing Along*, with music again by Martin Broones. Guy Bolton, Fred Thompson and Douglas Furber – all three experienced English writers of revue and musical comedy – provided the book, and lyrics were by Graham John, one of the wittier lyricists of his time. Leslie Henson and Fred Emney were in the cast.

Louise Browne had by this time become the Gaiety's leading lady – and if audiences probably came to see Leslie Henson, they went away talking too about Miss Browne, her singing, and above all her dancing – she was said to

Leslie Henson wagging an inebriated finger at an invisible Sydney Howard (the owner of the arm around Henson's shoulder) as they sang 'A Few Drinks' in *Funny Face* (1928).

be capable of over eighty consecutive *pirouettes* (though the improbability of this feat suggests that they were actually *fouettés*). *Swing Along* played happily through the Abdication crisis, and during eight months a seat could hardly be got.

On the night of the Coronation of George VI, the theatre took £406, a record for its entire life. The audience crowded in at 6.30, and the King's broadcast was relayed before the curtain went up. *Swing Along*, which had again been presented by Firth Shephard, ran for 311 performances; then Mr Shephard prepared *Going Greek*, which opened on September 16, 1937. The writers were the same; the music by a team of three American composers, the most accomplished of whom was Alan Jay Lerner.

Going Greek was performed, the playbills announced, by 'Leslie Henson and the Entire Gaiety Theatre Company' – a repertory company which included Louise Browne, Fred Emney and Richard Hearne. During years of obviously increasing international tension, it ran on until June 1938, doing even better business than Shephard's two previous shows. King George VI took Queen Elizabeth to the Gaiety during its run, and was seen to laugh heartily when Fred Emney asked Leslie Henson 'What is the Royal Mint?' and received the reply 'It's what the King puts over his roast lamb.' The general level of humour in the show may have been higher than that. Unfortunately it had to be taken off after 306 performances, when Leslie Henson was forced to leave the cast because of exhaustion.

On August 31, 1938, came the last first night at the Gaiety. Vivian Ellis had written the score of *Running Riot*; Debroy Somers once more led the theatre orchestra in the pit, and on-stage were the familiar figures – Leslie Henson, Louise Browne, Fred Emney and Richard Hearne, who in this show performed for the first time his now famous solo lancers, peopling the empty stage with invisible partners as he weaved the complex figures of the dance alone behind the footlights.

Though no-one knew for certain that this was the Gaiety's last show, there was a feeling of distinct unease: a plan for new traffic-ways approaching the new Waterloo Bridge had been announced, and it seemed that two theatres – the Gaiety and Irving's old Lyceum – were to be demolished to make way for widened roads. The Lyceum has survived as a *palais de danse*; perhaps in the end a more melancholy fate than that of the Gaiety, which at least still stands complete in the memory of now ageing theatre-goers.

It is pleasant that *Running Riot* was a success: but after six months, on the evening of February 25, 1939, the curtain fell for the last time on it and on the stage of the Gaiety. Many members of the audience had been at the last night of the old, original Gaiety Theatre, on July 4, 1903, and at the first night of George Edwardes' splendid new auditorium in October of the same year. Leslie Henson made a final speech, and they left – many of them taking ash-trays, binoculars, glasses from the bar, as souvenirs. Henson went home lugging with him the lamp from over the stage-door; Richard Hearne got a fire-bucket . . . .

Later, came the dismantling of the Gaiety; ironically, while buildings were destroyed all round it, the theatre, an empty shell, survived all the bombing of the Second World War – and the new approaches to Waterloo Bridge never materialised, so there was no need to demolish it. Just after the war, in 1946, Lupino Lane bought the building for £200,000 and three years later announced that the Ministry of Works had issued a permit to enable sufficient repairs to be carried out for him to be able to re-open the Gaiety, which he intended should once more become the home of musical comedy.

By June, 1950, he had spent £20,000 on tidying up the interior, but failed to raise an additional £100,000 to complete the refurbishing. On July 13, 1950, he announced that he had had to sell the site of the theatre for £180,000. A valedictory leading article appeared in *The Times*, and within weeks the old Gaiety had been demolished to make way for an office block – another office block. All that remains of the theatre is the gilt front of the gallery, the painted ceiling of the foyer, and a row or two of seats, which may be found in the Gaiety Bar on the first floor of the Victoria – a pub in Strathern Place, Bayswater.

Though the great years of the Gaiety had been in George Edwardes' time, it cannot be said that during its last half-century it had not had its successes or made its stars. Musical comedy history, perhaps, was made elsewhere – by Ivor Novello, just up the road at Drury Lane, and of course by the many invading American shows which took the town with their brilliant musicality and newly biting lyrics. But whenever musical comedy is mentioned, the Gaiety will be mentioned too. Together with Daly's, it preserved some of its magic through failure and half-failure – and preserved until the very last minute its own old tradition of musical comedy – until the doors were finally closed and its famous safety-curtain, with the portrait of the ideal Gaiety Girl in diaphanous draperies with a real jewel in the buckle of her belt and a real lamp in her hand, fell to the stage for the last time.

3

'The Maid' of Daly's

'I would like so much to have a part where one would be able to act . . . ' – PHYLLIS DARE

George Edwardes had built Daly's Theatre up into the friendly rival of his own Gaiety for the title of the best musical playhouse in London. Daly's had been built by the American impresario Augustin Daly on the site of a slum in Cranbourne Street – or Moll Flanders Parade – near Leicester Square. Mrs Squire Bancroft had christened the theatre, in 1891, by breaking a bottle of champagne against the foundation stone – injuring several passers-by with flying glass. Within ten years, the theatre was one of the two notable London homes of the musical play, its success crowned by the introduction to England of Lehar's *The Merry Widow* in 1907.

George Edwardes left Daly's in the possession of his eldest daughter, Mrs Sherbrooke, but in the hands of Robert Evett, a former actor and singer who eventually became its managing director. Evett had appeared in a large number of successful musicals – including some of the Savoy operas, *Merrie England*, and *The Merry Widow* – and might have been expected to have an eye and an ear for a good show.

His first enterprise at Daly's was a production of *The Happy Day*, a musical comedy written by Sir Seymour Hicks with music by Sidney Jones and Paul Rubens. The auguries were good. Seymour Hicks, apart from being a highly successful actor with an enormous range – he had not only appeared in musical comedy, but in straight plays and even on the halls – was the author of a very considerable number of plays. Sidney Jones had written the scores of *A Gaiety Girl*, *An Artist's Model*, *San Toy* and *The Geisha*, and Paul Rubens was simply one of the finest light music composers of his day.

His day did not, alas, last long. He had been born in 1876, and though he trained for the bar, never made much of an effort at anything but composition. In that field, however, his efforts were prodigious, and his output enormous: he wrote both book and lyrics of a number of his pieces, contributed single numbers to others (and no fewer than three to *Florodora*), and wrote incidental music for straight plays – for instance for Sir Herbert Tree's notable 1901 revival of *Twelfth Night*. His industry impressed even his fellow-composers. Sidney Jones once remarked that 'Paul could turn out a number while I'm taking off my hat and coat!'

The Happy Day was to be Rubens' last show, for he died the year after its production, aged only forty-one. It is often said that he died of a broken heart – that he had fallen desperately in love with Phyllis Dare, the beautiful star of musical comedy; that he travelled all over the country for three years to be near her, and that this exacerbated the tuberculosis which killed him. One of his best-known single numbers, 'I Love the Moon' (from *The Sunshine Girl*) was written to her.

His death was a great loss to musical comedy and to Daly's. At least his last show was a success. It opened on May 13, 1916, and ran for 241 performances, with José Collins in the lead, playing Camille Joyeuse, a lady whose character can be inferred from her name. It was Robert Evett who had signed Miss Collins to appear in London, after seeing her in the New York production of *The Merry Countess* (an adaptation of *Die Fledermaus*).

Born in London, she was the second daughter of the music-hall star Lottie Collins, who made the song 'Ta-ra-ra-boom-de-ay!' famous on the halls. After education in a convent school, she stepped on-stage for the first time when she was thirteen, as 'the Little Scotch Bluebell' in Harry Lauder's famous song 'I Love a Lassie'. By the time she was sixteen, she was an experienced performer, trained in the old school of five or six performances a night at different music-halls all over London. During the run of *The Merry Widow* at Daly's in 1907 she was signed up by George Edwardes to replace one of the cast, who was ill. She played for two evenings, and made a success of her one number; but for some reason it was cut from the score on the third night, and she was out of work. George Graves, who played Baron Popoff, used to tell how she dried her tears in his dressing-room, and said, 'Mr Graves, one day I'm coming back here, and when I do, it will be as a star.'

Though she played in a few musicals in London, it was only after she had been in America for a year that she was especially noticed in *The Merry Countess*. That was in 1912, when Evett saw her in New York; and even then she delayed, understandably making the most of her success there – appearing in *The Ziegfeld Follies*, *The Passing Show of 1914*, and in vaudeville, before coming home to London to play in *The Happy Day*.

It was the début of one of the great stars of the light musical theatre, and instantly recognised as a happy and promising one. Her splendid brunette beauty and her magnificently rich voice (shown off well in Rubens' music which, as more than one critic remarked, 'had operatic pretensions') won the audience immediately. *The Happy Day* was, certainly, a good setting for her: a great deal of money had been spent on it – 'beautiful, magnificent, brilliant, dazzling – all the old adjectives that used to be applied to productions at Daly's in George Edwardes' days', wrote one critic.

It was too long, running for four hours on the first night (Act I lasted for over an hour and a half, and contained two grand set-pieces for Miss Collins – 'song-scenas', as they were once called). It was also argued that 'the poor little story got lost in comic turns, songs, dances, choruses, processions . . .'. But few people complained. The theme of the piece was a popular one – an everyday story of Royal folk forced to marry, then falling in love with each other. And apart from José, there was Arthur Wontner, a handsome and experienced leading man, as Prince Charles of Galania, and two excellent comedians, G. P. Huntley (an admirable straight actor who for a while was to specialise in 'silly-ass' parts) and Lauri de Frece, one of whose ad-libs had given him the sad privilege of being able to claim that he had killed someone with laughter: an elderly gentleman in Bath laughed himself into a seizure at one of his jokes, and died of it.

In December, *The Happy Day* gave way to *Young England*, a play by Basil Hood, with music by G. H. Clutsam and Hubert Bath – 'A New Light Opera of Queen Elizabeth's Spacious Days', as the playbills put it. Mr Clutsam was, and remains, virtually unknown. Hubert Bath was a young man of promise – a Devonian ex-student of the Royal Academy of Music who had already composed a considerable amount of incidental music, and had been conductor of the Thomas Quinlan Opera Company, and at the Shaftesbury Theatre. Later he was to become conductor of the Carl Rosa Opera Company for whom he wrote a full-scale opera, *Bubbole*, in 1923. He wrote over 300 songs and choral works, and eventually composed for films.

Young England came to Daly's with a cast which included Hayden Coffin, Doris Woodall and Walter Passmore. Passmore was by way of being a shadow of George Grossmith, Senior, many of whose parts he assumed; he appeared in a large number of Savoy operas, and had become an excellent comedian. In *Young England* he played a character which had touches of Falstaff, Sir Toby Belch, and Osric! But it was the singing that mattered: there was a selection of choruses, together with an ambitious octet and a couple of quartets, all much admired. But the piece was caviar to the general, and did not run. On December 23, 1916 – ten days after the first performance of *Young England* in London – another musical comedy opened at the Prince's Theatre, Manchester, which would be brought into London if it was sufficiently well received. It *was* sufficiently well received. It was called *The Maid of the Mountains*.

The piece was said to be less an old-style musical comedy than 'a play told to a musical setting'. The Maid (José Collins) was the one woman among a band of brigands. Taken prisoner and held hostage in exchange for the leader of the band, with whom she was in love, she was rescued by him – only to become violently jealous when he fell in love with the Governor's daughter. Of course in the end he returned to the arms of the Maid; but there were sufficient romantic hesitations and tensions to fill out a good evening.

The Maid of the Mountains was cheered in Manchester, and when it opened at Daly's on February 10, 1917, the cheers redoubled – and indeed it was to

'Teresa's Farewell' – the scena which closed Act I of *The Maid of the Mountains* (1917): José Collins addressing the bandits. Note the stage rocks in the foreground, which Oscar Asche, producing, placed to deter his actors from coming downstage to sing 'at' rather than to the audience.

run for 1352 performances, and to make over £200,000 profit. It was to remain the second longest-running musical (next to *Chu Chin Chow*) for many years, until overtaken by *Me and My Girl* in the late 1930s.

The book had actually been written some time previously – by Frederick Lonsdale, a writer whose straight plays, *The Last of Mrs Cheyney* and *Canaries Sometimes Sing*, are sufficient evidence of his skill as a dramatist. Lonsdale alleged that he had started life as a runaway circus boy, a private soldier, a steward and a bellboy. He wrote his first play, he told people, because his landlady had threatened to throw him out of his lodgings for non-payment of rent. But his sophistication became a byword, and his characters, as one critic put it, 'make up in brightness and charm what they lack in significance as human beings.' *The Maid of the Mountains* lay around in Edwardes' office at Daly's for years, until Evett, faced with the fact that Edwardes' estate was in a far from stable condition, was searching for new and promising material.

Though Edwardes had had musicals running simultaneously at the Gaiety, Daly's, the Apollo, the Prince of Wales, and the Lyric, though four of his productions ran for over 700 performances, it was only at the Gaiety that he had been able to produce a run of profitable musicals. Within a year of his death, the bankruptcy of his estate seemed a distinct possibility.

It was under these conditions that Evett picked up the script of *The Maid of the Mountains*, saw some promise in it, and decided to take a gamble. He commissioned Harold Fraser-Simson to write the score, and persuaded José Collins to appear as the Maid for only £50 a week (she had been getting £500 a week in New York). It was in fact an economy production, with the simplest *dècor* and costumes, and the smallest possible chorus. Ironically, the economy paid off, for critics took it as a sign that the world of musical comedy was becoming more real, welcoming the fact that 'the note of the whole production is restraint and . . . freedom from whirlwind choruses and strident comedians.'

Miss Collins was joined, in the cast, by Arthur Wontner as the chief brigand, by Thorpe Bates (an admirable baritone with operatic experience), and Lauri de Frece (as excellent comic relief). They all had splendid material to work with: Lonsdale's dialogue was excellent, Fraser-Simson's score probably his best, and the various writers who provided lyrics also came up with some admirable work. Harry Graham, for instance, wrote the lyrics for the sweet waltz-song for Teresa, 'Love will Find a Way.'

What e'er befall
I still recall
That sunlit mountain side!
Where hearts are true
And skies are blue
And love's the only guide!
If faithful to my trust I stay
No fate can fill me with dismay!
Love holds the key to set me free
And love will find a way.

Oddly enough, perhaps the most popular number in the show was provided at a very late stage by José Collins's father-in-law, James W. Tate, who saw the try-out in Manchester, and suggested that one or two additional numbers might improve the piece. He locked himself in his room at the Midland Hotel, and emerged with three new songs. One of them, sung by Thorpe Bates at the London premiere, forced the conductor to disobey Evett's strict injunction that there were to be no encores. The audience simply would not stop cheering until Bates had repeated 'A

Bachelor Gay', for which the lyrics had been written by Clifford Harris and 'Valentine':

> A bachelor gay am I,
> Though I've suffered from Cupid's dart.
> But never I vow will I say die
> In spite of an aching heart.
> For a man always loves a girl or two;
> Though the fact must be confessed
> He always swears the whole way through
> To every girl he tries to woo
> That he loves her far the best . .
>
> At seventeen he falls in love quite madly
> With eyes of tender blue;
> At twenty-four he gets it rather badly
> With eyes of a different hue.
> At thirty-five you'll find him flirting sadly
> With two or three or more . . .
> When he fancies he is past love
> It is then he meets his last love,
> And he loves her as he never loved before.

Another of Tate's songs was 'A Paradise for Two'; but Fraser-Simson's waltz, his 'Live for Today' and 'Honour Among Thieves' ran them close.

The score remains redolent of the charm and tunefulness of its period: almost everything poor Fraser-Simson was to write ever afterwards was to be described as reminiscent of his score for *The Maid of the Mountains*. It was the sort of success a wise or lucky composer might wish for towards the end of his career. In a sense, Fraser-Simson peaked too early, in the modern phrase. But his score wears well: a revival of *The Maid of the Mountains* in the seventies, dated and musty though the book then seemed, was musically nothing but a joy.

The first production was far from musty in Oscar Asche's hands, and it made José Collins an absolute star. Seen and approved in *The Happy Day*, in *The Maid of the Mountains* she was acclaimed, not only for the beauty of her voice, but for her personality and acting ability. Appearing in a number of musicals and straight plays, and as a single variety act, she was to remain at the top of her profession for many years.

The possibility of following *The Maid of the Mountains* with a successful sequel was too tempting to disregard, and Fraser-Simson, assisted by Ivor Novello, wrote the score for a book by Dion Clayton Calthorp, setting lyrics by Harry Graham, Douglas Furber, and Adrian Ross. The result was *A Southern Maid*, again produced by Oscar Asche, which opened at Daly's on May 15, 1920, and ran for 306 performances.

There was, of course, a star part for José Collins; and the critics realised that the play was 'written around' her rather than as a dramatic story whose impetus was its own plot. 'She has scenes and situations which, if one did not see last week, one saw the week before, and will probably see the week after next', wrote one critic; and it was very fairly claimed that a happy ending which was entirely improbable had been spatchcocked in simply so that José Collins should not face a tragic end.

Considered at a distance, the score of *A Southern Maid* is not as inferior to that of *The Maid of the Mountains* as the critics of the time claimed. Certainly there is no single smash hit (though 'Love's Cigarette' has enormous period charm), but Fraser-Simson showed rather more technical accomplishment in the second score than the first. 'The Call of the Sea' and 'Bird of Blue' are numbers which would have been acclaimed in any other musical and from any other pen, while Ivor Novello's 'Every Bit of Loving' was evidently very winningly sung by Miss Collins. However, nothing could now protect Fraser-Simson from the accusation of re-writing *The Maid of the Mountains*: for the first, but certainly not the last time, 'strangely reminiscent' was the phrase most often used to describe his music.

Incidentally, one might pause for a moment to pay tribute to Douglas Furber, one of the lyricists of *A Southern Maid*. Lyric-writing is a very difficult skill, which few dramatists can command (though occasionally they have splendidly fortunate flukes, as P. G. Wodehouse did with his lyrics for 'Just My Bill'). Furber, in thirty years or so, wrote the lyrics for over seventy musical plays and revues, including ten Charlot revues and many Cochran shows, and worked too in Hollywood. His name crops up again and again in the history of musical comedy, to remind one of the important but neglected part played by the lyricists.

José Collins was by now Daly's most valuable property, and Evett would have been extremely foolish not to have seen the future in terms of a long series of pieces bought or commissioned especially for her. Alas, most of the best of them were to be by foreign composers. The first was *Sybil*, with music by Victor Jacobi. It was a pleasant score, and Evett cast the play strongly, with Harry Welchman and Huntley Wright to support Miss Collins.

Wright was no stranger to the theatre; he had appeared there continuously between 1896 and 1905, in (among other shows) *The Geisha*, *San Toy* and *The Cingalee*. He was a beautiful comedian, original and inventive, and a great favourite with the public. Harry Welchman's greatest successes were still ahead (most notably as Pierre Birabeau in *The Desert Song* in 1927) but already he was established as one of the best romantic leads musical comedy was to produce. (His last West End stage performance, over forty years later, was to be in *The World of Paul Slickey*, in 1959.)

Sybil ran for 346 performances; then Evett brought back *The Maid of the Mountains*, before producing *The Lady of the Rose*, adapted by Frederick Lonsdale from an Austrian original, with music by Jean Gilbert. Once again, one has to ask to what extent Lonsdale, an Englishman, contributed to the success of what was basically a continental piece. The answer must be that his contribution was considerable – but that the play can still hardly be called 'English' – and indeed it embraced many of the old Viennese conventions: Phyllis Dare, the star, made her entrance in the old Austrian manner, down a full staircase, clad in a magnificent gown. *The Maid of the Mountains* was already showing the way to a more realistic manner in the presentation of the musical play, and only Ivor Novello went on writing entrances of that sort, though one must also say that the audiences he commanded evidently loved that kind of thing.

Harry Welchman partnered Miss Dare (though for once as a villain), and her hero/lover was Roy Royston, the successful star of *The Boy*, and other musicals. Phyllis Dare, who had already had a long career since her first steps onto the stage of the Coronet Theatre, Notting Hill, in 1899, once gave vent to feelings which José Collins and other musical comedy stars must have shared:

> I find it a very monotonous and often tiresome life. The musical comedies themselves have not got much in them as a rule beyond songs and little scenes and conversations leading up to those songs. I would like so much to have a part where one would be able to act in a study of character, or at least feel that one was not repeating silly, empty words. And I have always got to be smiling.

She smiled on, for the time being, through 511 performances of *The Lady of the Rose*; then, in came a revival of *The Merry Widow*, with Evelyn Laye in the title-role, and with Carl Brisson (formerly, as Carl Pederson, welterweight boxing champion of Middle Europe) playing opposite her. This was a revival mounted by the new owner of Daly's, James White, who had bought the theatre for more than £200,000. 'Jimmy' White was not an easy man: he failed to get on with Evett, who left him to go to the Gaiety; and it was because of him that José Collins left Daly's, with the words 'You're going to come to a sticky end!' She was not wrong.

Born in comparative poverty, White became a millionaire by a series of speculations, the background of which remains obscure; he bought and sold theatres, cotton mills, stocks and shares . . . He claimed to have made over £750,000 in business in one day, and to have matched it by winning £100,000 in a single bet on the race-course. In 1900 he walked from London to Rochdale because he could not raise the fare. Not many years later, he was able to commission a special train to take him from London to Manchester. Now, he became besotted with Daly's, insisting on 'taking rehearsals' (which meant reducing them to chaos), and interfering with productions, rarely to their improvement.

A strange, unsympathetic, but deeply interesting figure, White killed himself in 1927, leaving a maudlin, self-pitying suicide note complaining obscurely about the activities of wealthy libertines and unscrupulous women. He was only forty-nine.

Lady Mary, with a score by Albert Sirmay and Philip Charig and a book by Frederick Lonsdale and J. Hastings Turner, which opened in February 1928, was the last real musical success at Daly's, and that was no tribute to the composers: the music was dismissed as being about as pleasant as dance music, and the story as extremely slight. What saved the show, and encouraged it to last for even so slender a run as 181 performances, was the presence in the cast of George Grossmith – always a draw.

Lonsdale had written *Lady Mary* especially for G. G. and announced the fact to him when they met one day for lunch at the Garrick Club. His part, 'Hatpin Pinge', was a good one – elegant, polished and witty, and dominating the piece despite the presence of Helen Gilliland, the pleasant Irish leading lady. Just over fifty, Grossmith no longer inevitably got the girl at the end of the evening, and was now more of a character comedian than he had been in the days of the old Gaiety successes. In *Lady Mary* he ambled through the evening doing a little singing, a little dancing, and always vastly entertaining the audience – which on one occasion included George V and Queen Mary. On another, King Amunullah of Afghanistan, despite the teetotal predilections of his countrymen, was entertained in the dressing-room in the interval with large quantities of whisky, and considerably delayed the rising of the curtain on Act II.

Now, alas, it was to be downhill all the way for Daly's. In February 1929, Harry Welchman brought *The White Camellia*, which he had been touring through the provinces, to Daly's under his own management. This was a romantic musical in the old tradition, written by Laura Leicester, with music by Pat Thayer and Arthur Wood (who had conducted at the Gaiety and Daly's). The show was very limply reviewed, and gave way after only two months to a revival of *The Lady of the Rose*, with Welchman, who also produced, in his old role.

Welchman learned a harsh lesson at Daly's, for he lost heavily on both his productions there, and at the end of the day announced that it had cost him £8000 to learn that 'musical comedy of the old-fashioned sort has no chance in 1929'. He also condemned the theatres in which musicals were then being presented: 'Rents are enormous, the seating is abominable, of comforts there are none. My advice is scrap the lot, and build some new ones.'

In May 1929, Daly's was offered for sale by private tender: the Westminster Bank had by then taken it over as creditors of 'Jimmy' White's estate. In June, it was bought by a South African millionaire, Isador M. Schlesinger, who at £250,000 outbid Edward Laurillard by £20,000. Laurillard might have saved the theatre; as it was, the building was dark until September 1930, when *Eldorado* was staged – proudly announced as 'an all-British production', with music by Rutland Clapham, whose name has passed from record. *Eldorado* was about a valuable diamond and its adventures, and *The Times* suggested that 'its sole distinction is to be found in the prettiness of its frocks and the admirable handling throughout each scene of shades of colour more delicate than we are accustomed to expect from designers of the musical comedy stage.' But the music seems to have been pleasant enough, and was at any rate sung brilliantly by one member of the cast – the leading lady, Desirée Ellinger, who had been a soloist with Sir Thomas Beecham's British National Opera Company, and had had the distinction of being able to auction a single kiss for £5 on 'Poppy Day'.

However, it seems that the one indisputable hit of the show on its first night was by an unlisted performer. The Act I curtain fell on a chorus grouped glumly around a heroine completely overcome by the pathos of a song entitled 'Love is Dead'. A stage hand rushed forward to hold back the curtain so that Miss Ellinger could walk through it to take her bow; but the management decided to raise it to show the final tableau once more. It rose, and the stage hand rose with it. Some feet above the ground, he let go, and landed on hands and knees at Miss Ellinger's feet, whereupon with a frightened look at the audience he crawled slowly off-stage to round after round of laughter and applause. *Eldorado* did not last long.

The next production, *Little Tommy Tucker*, had a score by Vivian Ellis, and a book by Desmond Carter, who turned the nursery rhyme into a modern parable with Thomasina Tucker as a cabaret star singing for other people's suppers. It had good tunes and a good book, lively lyrics, and the advantage of being one of the first shows in which Ralph Reader (later to be best known for his production of the Boy Scouts' Gang Shows) drilled the chorus; he was the first Englishman who realised, as Busby Berkeley did in films, the effect that could be achieved by treating a chorus as one of the stars of a show.

During 1931 and 1932 there was a long series of revivals at Daly's, but in July 1932 the theatre descended to non-stop variety, with performances from 2 p.m. to midnight at prices from one to five shillings. *Mother Goose*, in December 1932, was the first pantomime ever to be produced at the theatre, then came more revivals, and a number of straight plays.

That's a Pretty Thing, with music by Noel Gay, ran for a hundred or so performances from November 22, 1933. The book was by Stanley Lupino, but he did not appear, and the cast was a weak one. More straight plays – by P. G. Wodehouse, Sacha Guitry, R. C. Sherriff and others, led to the night of April 29, 1937, and the first night of the last musical to be produced at Daly's – an adaptation of that under-rated Offenbach operetta *The Grand Duchess of Gerolstein*. It ran for only two months, was replaced by *The First Legion*, a straight drama; and on September 25, 1937, the curtain fell for the last time on the stage of Daly's – to no special audience, and on no special occasion. Warner Brothers bought the building for £250,000, and built a cinema on its site. London had lost another piece of theatre history.

4

'Kissing Time' and the Twenties

'A thing of shreds and patches – but some of them were pretty shreds and gay patches.' – THE TIMES

In 1919, George Grossmith and Edward Laurillard had opened their new theatre, the Winter Garden, in Drury Lane. Out of uniform, 'G. G.' had looked around for a new theatre in which he and his partner could go into production – and production of musical comedies. He examined various derelict or almost derelict buildings – Sadler's Wells, the Marylebone, the Coronet – and then one day found himself outside the 'Old Mo', the Middlesex Music Hall in Drury Lane. The bills announced a French revue, with the most expensive seats at one-and-threepence. 'G. G.' ambled in, and liked the look of the place, though obviously it would need extensive refurbishing, new dressing-rooms, and other alterations. Its surroundings were not unduly salubrious – a pub on one side, a fish-and-chip shop on the other; but after all it *was* in Drury Lane, and the possibilities seemed considerable.

He went to see Sir Oswald Stoll, who owned it, and within a week he and Laurillard had bought the building, re-christened it the Winter Garden, and were planning the re-opening. It was a pleasant theatre – and though, with over 1800 seats, it held more people than His Majesty's, it seemed always to be a much more intimate house.

The refurbishing and reconstruction took some time. The opening show, too, was obviously important, and had to be thoroughly rehearsed – though rehearsals took place with scaffolding still up. Then a painters' strike delayed the first night. On the afternoon of May 20, 1919, Grossmith himself was wielding a paintbrush in the stalls. But that evening the curtain went up, before an enthusiastic and lively audience, on *Kissing Time*, a musical written by Guy Bolton and P. G. Wodehouse, and with music by Ivan Caryll.

It seemed a good choice. Bolton and Wodehouse had already worked together on a number of musicals, and had an easy, witty way with book and lyrics. Indeed, the work Wodehouse did in the musical theatre between the wars has been sadly under-rated: though most of it was done for American productions, his influence on English authors and lyricists was considerable.

Ivan Caryll had had his first great success in 1893, with *Little Christopher*

George Grossmith and Phyllis Dare in the waltz-duet 'There's a Light in your Eyes' from *Kissing Time* (1919), with which Grossmith opened his new theatre, The Winter Garden.

Columbus. *Kissing Time* was to be his last show: he died in 1921. He was, of course, in the pit on the first night, insisting as usual on the violinists in the orchestra tapping their fiddles with their bows when he appeared, then sitting stolidly on his conductor's chair and following every movement of the singers and dancers with his bright little black eyes. Earlier, he had added to the chaos in narrow Drury Lane by arriving at the theatre, as was his custom, in a pair-horse Victoria; most other people were by now in motor cars. It was a very fashionable audience: 'G. G.' was a great favourite, and apart from looking forward to seeing him playing the hero of a play produced in his own theatre, they looked forward too to the rest of the cast: Leslie Henson, Stanley Holloway, Isabel Jeans, Tom Walls, Phyllis Dare, Yvonne Arnaud . . .

That first-night audience cheered everyone and everything: it was a happy-go-lucky evening, reminiscent of the good old days at the Gaiety. Indeed, one might almost have thought one was *at* the Gaiety, for several of the members of its front- and back-stage staff had followed 'G. G.' up the road to the new theatre, including his housekeeper Maggie Foster, whose main job was to keep unwanted visitors out of his dressing-room. She was something of a snob, and delighted in announcing the more distinguished visitors – 'The Very Reverend the Dean of Barchester', or 'The Right Honourable the Chancellor of the Exchequer'. But her welcome did not extend to members of 'G. G.' 's own profession, who got a somewhat mumbled introduction: 'Sir John Hare of the Garrick Theatre – I believe', or 'Mr George Graves – just back from the provinces'.

'G. G.' 's instinct was right: *Kissing Time* was a success, and ran for 430 performances, critics and public alike particularly enjoying Phyllis Dare, 'now in the front rank of musical comedy heroines', in her most successful number, 'Some Day'.

Before the Winter Garden opened its doors with *Kissing Time*, there were a few other enjoyable shows to be seen and heard in the West End. There was *Valentine*, for instance, which was produced at the St James's in January 1918, with music by Napoleon Lambelet – an Englishman by adoption, for though born in Corfu he conducted at a large number of London theatres. His were 'real tunes, if a little on known lines', said a critic; there was a well-designed ballet, and the star was Marjorie Gordon, with Hayden Coffin and Doris Dean (who 'has for her vocation to make love to anybody who happens to be for the moment neglected, and to her audience when all else fails'). It sounds a show which was probably mildly entertaining to anyone who dropped in; though these were not many, for it had been taken off by April 20, and has vanished almost without trace from the annals.

In some cases it is difficult to imagine that the story of a musical comedy could seriously have engaged composer and writer. *Flora*, which was presented at the Prince of Wales in March 1918, was apparently about a wealthy but vulgar family intent on marrying its daughters into the peerage, and about a gardener who came into a fortune just as the rich snob father had lost his. Well, *Punch* at this period was full of rather ill-mannered jokes at the expense of the *nouveau riche,* and Harry Grattan, who wrote *Flora*, had written a number of good revues, so the book may have been more than acceptable to the average audience. And the half-dozen composers associated with it (including Frederick Norton and Max Darewski) had written a sprinkling of bright, if not remarkable songs.

The cast was led by Gertie Millar and Joe Nightingale – the latter had made his reputation two years previously as Willie Mossop, the gormless cobbler in Harold Brighouse's splendid *Hobson's Choice*; the former had been George Edwardes's great star, playing at the Gaiety for eight years as a leading lady, and later at Daly's. She was the girl to whom, truly, the mashers and stage-door johnnies paid tribute – and Edwardes gave her permission to leave the theatre by the front entrance, in order to avoid the crowds which would gather at the stage door after each performance. *Flora* is a show one would be pleased to have seen, even if its run was short.

In 1918, musical comedy still occasionally made reference to wartime conditions, and if it got them right, got a laugh. In *Violette* (which opened at the Lyric in May) the action took place in the Kingdom of Celaria in 1818 – but four meat coupons were still offered as a bribe to a sentry (dressed in a cream-and-crimson uniform and with a cockade in his cap!) John Ansell, who wrote the score, was musical director of a rival theatre, the Alhambra – and in 1926 was to be appointed conductor of the 2LO Wireless Orchestra. Violet Essex and Beatrice Hunt made a success of some of the songs, which were melodious and, 'not too reminiscent'.

An unexpected name leaps off the page of the reference books when one comes across *Soldier Boy*, which played at the Apollo from June 26, 1918 – one of the authors was the thriller-writer Edgar Wallace, who collaborated with Rita Johnson Young to produce a book about a French Army officer who takes the place of a comrade reported missing in battle, so that his blind mother and his sister will be spared the bad news. It will come as no surprise to learn that he falls in love with the sister, but that the dead man turns up happily healthy by the time the two are united at the final curtain. Critics found the war 'a strange background for a musical comedy', but did not seem unduly put out by the presence of a handsome 'beauty chorus'. Anyway, the songs by Samuel Rombeau and Frederick Chapelle were enjoyable, and enjoyably sung. (Chappelle is a misty figure; Rombeau seems to have been a less than fully occupied civil servant, employed in the Savings Bank Department – for besides simultaneously teaching mathematics and chemistry, he found time to write the scores of two dozen musicals and several films.)

The success of *Chu Chin Chow* inevitably attracted imitations. *Shanghai* was an obvious attempt to cash in on that success. Produced at Drury Lane in August 1918, it was really a pantomime based on the story of Aladdin – 'a thing', *The Times* said, 'of shreds and patches, but some of them were pretty shreds and gay patches.' The star of the piece was Alfred Lester, the splendidly lugubrious comedian, who does not seem to have been entirely sure of the dramatic viability of the play: watching as the hero, a young Chinese nobleman condemned to death, was being lengthily brave while saying farewell to his mistress, Lester turned to the audience and dryly remarked 'What a film this would make!' And an hour or so later, apparently tiring of the piece (in which he played Hu Du, a Bringer of Misfortune), he shambled off-stage through the auditorium, turning to survey his colleagues and remark 'Now I come to look at you, you're not a bit like Chinese, after all.' It all sounds much more like pantomime than anything else; but the score for *Shanghai* was treated seriously by Isidor Witmark, who nevertheless only succeeded in producing one really successful number – for 'The Wiggle-Woggle', a dance energetically performed by Bert Coote and Joan Hay. And even that has now perished from the memory.

Shanghai ran for 131 performances, and seems to have been 'nursed' by the Drury Lane management. Other theatres could not afford to make a brave show of things by packing the house with complimentary tickets – or not for too long, anyway. And there were, alas, a good number of failures. There was, for instance, in 1920, *Pretty Peggy*, a sort of amalgam of a Drury Lane pantomime, a Lyceum melodrama, and an old-fashioned burlesque. It was written by Arthur Rose and Charles Austin – the latter a great star of the music-halls, whose 'Parker, P. C.' was a character he took with him, slightly disguised, into *Pretty Peggy*. The music was by A. Emmett Adams, an unknown composer, but Austin was the attraction and, *The Times* reported, made the audience laugh for three hours sans intermission. Lorna and Toots Pounds, a popular couple, had an equal success with a burlesque of Oscar Asche and Lily Brayton in *Chu Chin Chow*.

In April 1920, *The Little Whopper* opened at the Shaftesbury. A considerable amount of money was obviously spent on mounting this show; but it failed, as a very great number of musical comedies have failed, not so much because of the weakness of the score (though indeed that seems to have been of strong natural insignificance) as because of the lack of good material for even so excellent a comedian as Davy Burnaby.

Cherry, which opened at the Apollo on July 22, 1920, had perhaps more of a chance: it was a coster musical comedy, in which Marie Blanche (once the wife of the inestimably handsome Lewis Waller) got wonderful notices for discarding her usual stately air – she was a famous principal boy of Drury Lane pantomime – to play a coster girl born and bred, with characteristic quick repartee, boisterous good humour, and love of fair play. *The Times* was especially pleased with her: 'She shows herself possessed of a power of characterisation which comes as a surprise even to those who have seen a good deal of her work', wrote its critic.

But the Pygmalion-like story of a girl who works in a jam factory, is snatched away to an aristocratic world, but breaks off her engagement to a young peer to return to her hawker boy-friend, only lasted for two months. In musical-comedy, audiences had a strong preference for never-never land; that kind of thing might be alright, eight years earlier, for Bernard Shaw – but the musical stage had to wait another twenty-five years before accepting it as a theme.

A number of musicals were only partly British in origin, and so outside the scope of this book. Emmerich Kálmán, for instance, was the foreign composer of *The Little Dutch Girl,* which opened at the Lyric on December 1, 1920; even if the book was by Seymour Hicks and the lyrics by Harry Graham, it can scarcely be described as a 'British' musical comedy. It ran for 207 performances, with Jack Hulbert as its principal comedian – but the really interesting thing about it was that Maggie Teyte, the singer whom Debussy chose to sing Mélisande in *Pélleas and Mélisande,* played its heroine – the Grand Duchess of Sylvania. She marries the Crown Prince of Sarragon in the morning, dashes over to Holland to fall in love with him in person in the afternoon, and returns to her palace in time for a reconciliation before dinner. The production gave Hulbert a major triumph, too – and was the play in which he first elaborated his splendid habit of holding perfectly incoherent but apparently intelligent conversations with himself.

In March 1921 came one of the brightest successes of the decade, as far as British musical plays are concerned – the production at the Empire of *The Rebel Maid*. It was a romantic light opera with a hero and heroine both (unknown to each other) plotting to help William of Orange against King James.

The music was by Montague Phillips, who heard his score cheered on the first night – as indeed it deserved, for it was ambitious in its way, with a beautiful quartet in the first act ('Shepherdess and Beau Brocade') and good single numbers: 'I Want my Man to be a Landlord' for Betty Chester, 'The Knife Grinder' for Walter Passmore, and – the only number to have survived until this day – 'The Fishermen of England' sung by Thorpe Bates, formerly a concert bass, who thundered it out to such effect that the encores seemed likely to put a permanent end to the performance. Clara Butterworth, Montague Phillips' wife, appeared as the 'rebel maid'.

Apart from the single numbers, the chorus was especially praised by the critics for its energy and enthusiasm, especially in a second-act closing number which left the theatre buzzing with excitement during the interval. Even if the triumphant appearance of William of Orange went a little damply ('confirming an impression that some have long held that he was the forerunner of Captain Hook', said one critic), the evening was nothing if not successful.

Two more British musicals opened during 1921, competing with Jerome Kern's *Sally* at the Winter Garden and Kálmán's *Gypsy Princess* at the Prince of Wales. The first was *My Nieces*, which opened at the Queen's on August 19 to the disheartening sound of boos from the gallery. The gallery was right: a careless adaptation of Pinero's *The Schoolmistress*, it made mincemeat of the witty original text, and while the music by Howard Talbot was 'charming', and Binnie Hale was greeted by *The Times* as 'a perfect artist', the evening was deadly slow. But the investment was not lost: quickly refurbished with new songs by Philip Braham and with new dances choreographed by Jack Buchanan, the show was transferred to the Aldwych and succeeded in running for 172 performances, covering its production costs.

Now and Then, which was staged at the Vaudeville in mid-September, demonstrated the dangers of such newfangled toys as the telephone, for George Graves, the principal character, received an electric shock from that obviously unreliable instrument which promptly dispatched him (in his dreams) three hundred years through time to the court of Queen Elizabeth I. Mr Graves, playing a 'match king', took the opportunity to impress the Queen by making fire – but found to his distress that the only matches he had about his person were safety matches, and without the necessary box on which to strike them. Meanwhile, there was a heroine (Joyce Barbour) who scandalised the court by dancing a gavotte which gradually turned into a foxtrot with a display of high kicks, and there was the arrival on-stage of William Shakespeare (played by Miles Malleson) to whom the match king, was able to give a little advice on the construction of his latest comedy, to be called *Hamlet*.

André Charlot, the admirable producer of successful revues, mounted *Now and Then*, and perhaps for that reason it was billed as 'a musical extravaganza'; but it was obviously nearer the format of musical comedy than revue. Philip Braham wrote the score.

1922 was a bad year: the only really notable piece was *The Smith Family* at the Empire, starring Harry Tate, the music-hall comedian, in a frolic about a man engaged to make a foreign Prince laugh, who hadn't so much as smiled since the day he was born. It ran for just over one hundred performances. *The Island King*, at the Adelphi the same year, lasted for sixty performances longer – but this was mainly because of the presence of W. H. Berry, who played a petty officer suffering from 'bottle-ism', who was transplanted to the South Sea Islands as a king. Dorothy Shale sang Harold Garstin's music very prettily; but it was Berry who kept the piece running. He had, it was said, never been funnier.

Neither was 1923 exactly a brilliant year, though *Head Over Heels* once more starred the ubiquitous W. H. Berry – unhappily cast as a circus tumbler suddenly placed in charge of a circus, and bound also to pretend to be the heir to a dukedom (for reasons which escape one even after a reading of the book). Berry presided uneasily over an Adelphi stage full of animals – dogs, a donkey, a horse, and an elephant ('of sorts', said *The Times* disparagingly). Seymour Hicks had written the piece, and Harold Fraser-Simson the music ('tuneful but reminiscent', was the inevitable reception of the score); Dennis Noble, that splendid Rigoletto, Valentine, Figaro, Sharpless – better known at Covent Garden than the Adelphi – lent his marvellously pure and powerful baritone to the production; but to little avail. Mainly because of Berry, the piece lasted for 113 performances.

The other 1923 show was *Almond Eye*, which opened at the New Scala in December – on Boxing Day, in fact, which seems suitable, for the piece was described as 'an Eastern production of a very expensive type'. It was Aladdin-up-to-date, with Lilian Davies as a modern Princess Balroulbadour with far too few songs, and involved in a plot which unfolded with quite astonishing slowness. Frederick Rosse's music was pleasant, but spread very thinly; 'when the action is stopped for the intrusion of a song', complained the *Tatler*, 'all the characters are straining at the leash to begin their sermonising again'. The piece flopped to a close in no time.

The year 1924 opened with *Kate, or Love Will Find a Way*, described as 'a fantastical ballad-opera', at the Kingsway on February 25, which sent audiences away from the first night, one critic wrote, 'with a riot of good tunes in the head'. They weren't, in fact, the tunes of Gerard Williams, who had simply repeated the trick of *The Beggars' Opera* and arranged his score from folksongs and other Old English sources, using the original lyrics as well.

It followed a respectable convention, and on the first night seemed to have paid off: it was an extremely happy evening, beginning with May Day dances and Jack-on-the-Green, and ending on board H.M.S. *Chimera* with a sea shanty and 'Rule, Brittania!' In between, there had been true love in distress, jolly Jack Tars, pretty girls, comic villains, smugglers and press-gangs. And 'every time anyone does anything, and often when nobody does anything', *The Times* wrote, 'Mr Gerard Williams brings up one of those fresh old tunes, so much fresher than the tunes of today, and embroiders it with happy little quips of orchestration.'

Other critics were equally enthusiastic. But the public, alas, was not, and what was certainly a successful musical play was withdrawn after only four weeks – another piece of evidence in the continual argument about the relative meaning of the word 'success'.

The Street Singer, Harold Fraser-Simson's and Frederick Lonsdale's newest offering, opened at the Lyric on June 27. *The Street Singer* had a cast led by Phyllis Dare and Harry Welchman, and in it Miss Dare disguised herself in order to befriend the spineless hero, who happened to be 'the greatest painter in France'. The *Illustrated London News* had its doubts about his success in the world of Matisse and Klee, having seen some specimens of his work in the first act. But perhaps, the critic kindly suggested, there were some more mature works hidden in the cellar?

Lonsdale's book was intelligent and witty, and told what story there was with considerably more succinctness than most writers in the *genre* could command. But yes, Mr Fraser-Simson's score was again 'tuneful, yet somewhat reminiscent'. Still, the piece ran for 360 performances, which was a great deal better than average.

The only other British work of the 1924 season was *Patricia*, which went into His Majesty's at the end of October. Geoffrey Gwyther, who had appeared in *Chu Chin Chow*, composed the music – his only full-length score. But the song most loudly cheered by the audience on the opening night was 'For He's a Jolly Good Fellow', which was lustily sung by cast and chorus at the Prime Minister, Mr Baldwin, who appeared in a stage box. What Mr Baldwin thought of the plot, in which Dorothy Dickson discovered that her husband really loved her after all, and sang and danced about it at great length, is not revealed; but the piece only ran for 160 performances, so perhaps it was not all that engaging. One does not suppose that this worried Baldwin, who had just won a towering electoral victory for the Tories on the basis of the forged Zinoviev letter.

Harry Welchman played the lead in *Love's Prisoner*, which he produced. It was set in Cornwall, a county he dearly loved, and to which he retired at the end of his career. The stage of the Adelphi must have borne a distinct resemblance to the stage of the Savoy half a century earlier, for not only was the piece full of pirates, but there was actually a trio in Act II which started with the words 'With Cat-Like Tread'. The music, by Reginald Hargreaves, was not as good as Sullivan, but there were nevertheless several good numbers, including a 'Goodnight' chorus for fishermen and maids, half folk-song and half lullaby, which is really quite charming. The plot – deep, romantic and necessarily tangled – was more melodrama than musical comedy, involving an officer of Napoleon's army who was held prisoner in Cornwall and planned to escape so as to reveal the whereabouts of a hidden treasure to the little corporal. Helen Gilliland and Welchman made the most of it all; but to no avail. The play only ran for twenty-eight performances.

W. H. Berry took the stage of His Majesty's in March 1925 with *Bamboula*, a weak imitation of *The Island King*, in which he was once more a native ruler – this time of Corona, a state threatened by bizarre plots and counter-plots. Rather as in the former piece, he saved the show while he was on-stage; when he was off, it became extremely tedious – although Harry Welchman as a 'dance-poodle' (a dancing instructor) who eventually became a first-rate constitutional monarch, was not at all bad. The notices were stolen by Mimi Crawford, who sang and danced beautifully; but the piece did not have much of a run.

Betty in Mayfair, based on the successful *Lilies of the Field*, was another score by Harold Fraser-Simson (the music was 'often reminiscent', said *The Times*). It ran for 182 performances, with Evelyn Laye as one twin daughter of a Vicar being rather outplayed by Mary Leigh, as the less important daughter, but the more vivid character. That opened at the Adelphi on November 11. A week later at the Duke of York's, *Nicolette* opened, proudly announced as 'all-British'. One would never have guessed: it was set in the state of Volania, which had a Balkan atmosphere with touches of Spain and Italy. The President of Volania was dressed as a central European in Act II, and as a participant in the American Civil War in Act III. The plot was nebulous, and 'a mixed reception' was reported on the first of its twenty-eight nights.

In September 1926, came a rather extraordinary evening at the Adelphi. Herman Finck, a Londoner who had started his career as pianist in the pit of the Palace Theatre in 1892, and rose to be its musical director for over twenty years, wrote the score with Joseph Meyer for *Merely Molly* to a book by J. Hastings Turner, the author of *The Lilies of the Field*. The entertainment had attracted the attention of one of the finest actors of his time, and some would say the greatest Othello of his generation, Godfrey Tearle. He played the Duke of Wynninghame, who married for the sake of her reputation Molly Shine, a Stepney work-girl. James Agate, whose love of musicals was something short of complete, attended the first night for *The Sunday Times*.

'Now I am not going to pretend that I derive the same amount or quality of pleasure from Mr Tearle's Duke of Wynninghame that I do from his Othello; but I am not going to deny that his performance is very delightful in its way. The actor accomplishes the climb-down with all possible dignity.' For once, the piece had a good sense of period:

> Dock Lane, Stepney, was a setting of most excellent realism, including door numbers of the correct shape, and imitation silk stockings with authentic cotton tops and trade marks unobliterated by the laundry. It was a pity, one thinks, not to complete the observance of verisimilitude by an invitation to the Stepney roughs to discard their massive gold signet rings.

Among the other players Agate admired were Max Wall, making his first London appearance, and about to undergo years of neglect before his peculiar genius was recognised, and Evelyn Laye, who had 'abandoned the entire caboodle of artificiality and mannerism for the altogether more sensible business of acting'.

In September 1927 came *The Beloved Vagabond* – not, alas, anywhere near the realism of *Merely Molly*, even visually; Old Uncle Paragot took down his fiddle from the wall to tell the story of the Bohemian poet who loved the English lady, and how Blanquette waited for him through years of hopeless love and achieved him in the end – though he never forgot the beautiful Joanna. The hero, played by Frederic Ranalow, an Irish singer whose greatest success had been as Macheath in the famous revival of *The Beggar's Opera* at the Lyric, Hammersmith, 'had little to sing that was worth singing, but neither had anyone else' (said *The Sunday Times*). Even Lilian Davies' three expensive and striking dresses failed to preserve the show for more than a moderately respectable 107 performances.

Britain, in 1928, produced nothing to rival the success of Jerome Kern's *Show Boat* at Drury Lane. *Virginia*, by Jack Waller and Herbert Clayton, which opened at the Palace in October (five months after the opening of *Show Boat*), almost looks like an attempt to cash in on the success of the American show, for it was all Negro songs in the cottonfields, and roses round the door. In fact it was rather different, with George Gee as the secret husband of an American millionaire's daughter who should have been married to a peer. The Negro choruses went down well, décor and costumes were attractive, and some of the songs – notably 'Roll Away, Clouds' – were moderately well received.

The worthiest musical play of 1928 remains extremely interesting: to a book by Clemence Dane (who also wrote the lyrics), Richard Adinsell wrote the music for *Adam's Opera*, which was produced at the Old Vic in December. It was a re-working of the story of the Sleeping Beauty – but when the Princess (Adèle Dixon) was awakened by the Prince, it was to find that he had less than complete faith in her; he was stoned to death by her and her court before she fell asleep again.

It was a serious attempt to examine the recurrent appearance in the world of men or demi-gods who, said to be 'before their time', were at first welcomed and then rejected. Miss Dane, an admirable dramatist and novelist, had turned out an extremely intelligent book, and lyrics that aspired to the condition of poetry:

> I met a pretty singing lass
> As lovely as could be:
> She looked into a scrying glass
> To know her destiny.
> She hoped for a lover,
> She looked for a friend,
> She saw but her own face
> World without end.

Rather better than your average musical comedy foof; and so was Adinsell's music, which relied heavily on simple nursery rhymes, with modern allusions ('The Red Flag', for instance) woven into the texture. The tunes for the most part avoided deliberate originality, though they were given modern harmonic treatment, and jazz was used sparingly (and perhaps a little uneasily) at appropriate moments. The piece was not a commercial success, being too light for the highbrows and too original for the middlebrows.

Little enough remains of the twenties, if one excepts *Bitter Sweet* (to be examined in the next chapter). There were only two musicals in 1929 – the first, *Merry, Merry* (in February at the Carlton) once more starring W. H. Berry, and that sad comedian A. W. Bascomb. It ran for 131 performances without being in the least notable.

Dear Love, a sentimental piece which opened at the Palace in November, at least had the virtue of having Sydney Howard and Claude Hulbert in the cast – enough to keep an audience happily amused; Annie Croft and Tom Burke played the leads. What plot there was concerned Suzanne, who must marry a man of title or forfeit a huge fortune. So, heavily veiled, she married a titled Bohemian painter, engaged for a generous fee; only, of course, to fall deeply in love with him later, and to sing with him several sugary duets written for the occasion by Haydn Wood, the violinist and composer whose 'Roses of Picardy' is a nostalgic passport to a certain immortality. In *Dear Love*, *The Times* suggested that he managed skilfully to avoid mawkishness.

There was an enormous chorus, a genuinely gay and lively opening scene, a beautiful silver ballet in a brown salon, and a happy episode in a bright and sunny courtyard. The play ran for 132 performances, which was about right for it; and with it, an account of the miscellaneous musicals of the twenties can end, without, unfortunately, any creditable climax. Except that on the stage of His Majesty's, in 1929, swept a show which promised to lift the British musical play out of the slough. It was *Bitter Sweet*, and its author was Noël Coward.

5

Noël Coward

'Who doesn't love his youth? For that is what Coward is . . . *Private Lives*, *Conversation Piece*, *Operette*, *Tonight at 8.30*, and all those songs we sang to our girls driving back in the red MG from the Thames pub on a summer night in 1936.' – JOHN WHITING

The idea for *Bitter Sweet* – or at any rate for a romantic operetta – is said to have occurred to Noël Coward one evening when a recording of *Die Fledermaus* had started him thinking about the *genre*, and in particular about the 'sweet' old musical comedies he had seen as a boy at Daly's. He and his friend, the designer Gladys Calthrop, began talking about the idea during a car journey, and by the end of it their minds were full of the lilt of waltz-time, and images of men in uniform and beautiful women in magnificent gowns.

Coward scribbled down the rough outline of *Bitter Sweet* while on the voyage home after a visit to America with C. B. Cochran, the impresario, looking for talent for the New York production of *This Year of Grace*. He wrote the highly romantic and most successful Act II, set in Schlick's Café in Vienna, first – while in a nursing home recovering from a most unromantic operation, for piles. While appearing in his revue in New York a few weeks later, he managed substantially to finish the book and the outline of the score, and in London in 1929 the show went into rehearsal with Peggy Wood and Ivy St Helier as Sari Linden and Manon la Crevette. The male lead was more difficult: Coward and Cochran went to Vienna to search for a leading man, and found a handsome and magnificent young tenor who would have been ideal. His name, however, was Hans Unterfucker, and they decided that its appearance on the billboards might lead to comment in the West End. Eventually, back in London, George Metaxa was engaged.

Cochran never had any doubt of the operetta's success. 'I've got an old-age pension', he announced happily to the general manager of Drury Lane, after he had heard the piece for the first time. In Manchester, where the try-out opened in July 1929, people stood on their chairs to cheer. In London, at His Majesty's, two weeks later, the first night fell short of complete triumph: it was one of those 'fashionable' first nights, with Royalty present, during which the audience is more sure of its own success than of the virtues of the play. The lack of a chorus-line, and the fact that the girls in

Peggy Wood as Sarah and George Metaxa as her singing-master Carl Linden in a scene from Noël Coward's *Bitter-Sweet* (1931). 'Now Miss Sarah, if you please, Sing a scale for me . . .' was the preamble to the show's greatest hit, 'I'll See You Again'.

Bitter Sweet had been chosen more for their voices than their looks, did not help; and Coward and Gladys Calthrop were forced to help things along by repairing to the gallery to shout 'Cochran! Cochran!' while he, at the back of the circle, shouted 'Author! Author!'

The notices next morning were restrained – though James Agate, on the following Sunday in *The Sunday Times*, recognised that the score was 'cultivated, deft, witty, and, above all, tuneful', that 'Ladies of the Town' could have gone into any comic opera ever written and not be ashamed, and that 'Mr Coward shows himself to be possessed of the triple gift of your true man of the theatre – the faculty for entertaining both the eye, the ear and the mind.'

The whole production, he said, was 'a thundering job. If anybody can do the same sum and make more of it, let him come forward! He won't have any difficulty in getting a theatre; all the theatres will be tumbling over each other to get him. Of course, the whole country is teeming with people who are capable of doing what Mr Coward has done. Only nobody else has done it yet. Nobody else has ever done it, except Wagner. And *Meistersinger* is not strictly an operetta.'

The public loved *Bitter Sweet*, from the start. It ran for 697 performances, transferring to the Palace Theatre during its run, then going out to Streatham Hill and Golder's Green before returning to the West End to play thirty-two more performances at the Lyceum.

Coward entitled his play *Bitter Sweet: an Operette*; and while he called his other musicals 'a musical play' or 'a musical romance', there is no doubt that his first success is indeed right in the tradition of operetta. Its plot alone underlines the fact: the Marchioness of Shayne, an elderly hostess, tells her guests the story of her life. Peggy Wood shed fifty years after the first scene, to appear as Sarah Millick, a sixteen-year-old girl having a singing lesson from the handsome Carl Linden, with whom, of course, she is in love: 'Singing scales will never be so sweet again', she sings, and they sail into Coward's best-known and best-loved song, 'I'll See You Again.'

Sarah rejects her stuffy fiancé, to run away with Carl. In Vienna, she encounters Manon la Crevette, Carl's former mistress, and rejects the advances of the young Captain August Lutte. But she is by now working as a professional dance hostess, and is forced to dance with him. When he kisses her passionately, Carl, leading the orchestra at the time, strikes him, is challenged to a duel, and killed. Fifteen years later, the well-known opera star Madame Sari Linden has been invited to sing at a party held by Lord Shayne in London. She arrives: and her old friends recognise – Sarah.

Back in 'the present', the Marchioness of Shayne (for of course she accepted a proposal of marriage from Lord Shayne) has finished her story. A young girl who has been hesitating whether to marry her dull young fiancé, or run away with her lover, a musician, decides for the latter. In a compulsively theatrical final *scena*, the lover plays 'I'll See You Again' as a fox-trot, everyone dances off-stage, and Lady Shayne, laughing 'a strange, cracked, contemptuous laugh', holds out her arms and sings the final *reprise*:

> Though my world has gone awry,
> Though the end is drawing nigh,
> I shall love you till I die,
> Good-bye!

Many of Coward's single numbers, for revue or for musicals, are more brilliant verbally and perhaps musically than anything in *Bitter Sweet*. But the complete score is still his best: 'Ladies of the Town', 'If Love Were All' (Ivy St Helier's great success), 'Little Café', 'Tokay!' (the splendid chorus for officers which opens Act II, scene ii); 'Kiss Me', and 'Zigeuner' are all first-rate. 'Green Carnations', sung in the third act by a quartet of effete young men, satirised the aesthetes of the nineties, and was still daring enough to provoke some protests in the twenties.

Coward the lyric-writer, indeed, was also at his best – not only in the wittier numbers, but in the romantic songs, and perhaps especially in the wry number for Ivy St Helier as Manon:

> Life is very rough and tumble
> For a humble *diseuse*;
> One can betray one's troubles never
> Whatever occurs.
> Night after night, have to look bright
> Whether you're well or ill;
> People must laugh their fill.
> You mustn't sleep till dawn comes creeping.
> Though I never really grumble
> Life's a jumble indeed –
> And in my efforts to succeed
> I've had to formulate a creed –
>
> I believe in doing what I can,
> In crying when I must, in laughing when I choose.
> Heigh-ho, if love were all I should be lonely.
> I believe the more you love a man,
> The more you give your trust,
> The more you're bound to lose:
> Although when shadows fall I think if only
> Somebody splendid really needed me,
> Someone affectionate and dear,
> Cares would be ended if I knew that he
> Wanted to have me near.
> But I believe that since my life began
> The most I've had is just a talent to amuse.
> Heigh-ho, if love were all . . .

Incidentally, A. P. Herbert was surely somewhat justified when he

Manon la Crevette (Ivy St Helier), a girl of 'a certain type', sings to Austin Trevor while Clifford Heatherley looks on at Schlick's Café in Vienna: a scene from *Bitter-Sweet*.

criticised Coward's freedom in rhyming: anyone who rhymes *diseuse* with *occurs* either has something seriously wrong with his ear or is over-impatient to get the job done! However, that is by the by: *Bitter Sweet* is perhaps the best show of its kind to have been produced between the wars, and it is astonishing that there has been no good professional revival of it recently.

The two films made of it were more or less disastrous – one, directed by Herbert Wilcox in 1933 (with Anna Neagle as Sari) was not saved even by Miss St Helier's recapitulation of her stage role. The 1941 MGM version for Nelson Eddy and Jeannette MacDonald not only altered the plot, but reassigned most of the musical numbers to one or other of those two stars, and rearranged Coward's score, providing additional lyrics by Gus Kahn! A quarter of a century later an astonished Coward was to receive a message from Jeannette MacDonald: she had been performing *Bitter Sweet* on stages all over the U.S., appropriating Manon's 'If Love Were All' to herself, and inserting 'Mad About the Boy' into the score, and could she please present her production on Broadway? No, gasped the author.

But by then, *Bitter Sweet* was secure in the hearts of the million theatre-goers who had seen it on stage, and of millions more who knew the music from recordings made by the original cast, and eventually by many other artistes. Even advertisers had cottoned on: Robertson's marmalade launched a new Bitter-Sweet Marmalade, which Peggy Wood was said to find 'yummy'. Produced in New York with Evelyn Laye, the piece was a triumphant success: seats for the first night exchanged hands for $150 (then over £30) each, the audience cheered Miss Laye when she made her entrance in the last act, and the show played to $55,000 a week at the height of the Wall Street crash. All in all, over the years, it made for Coward something over a quarter of a million pounds. Who would argue that the prize was over-generous?

Coward had written his first song when he was only seventeen – a little number entitled 'Forbidden Fruit', with, even then, some typical Coward lines:

> Every peach
> Out of reach
> Is attractive . . .

Unlike Ivor Novello, who had an early and enormous success with 'Keep the Home Fires Burning', Coward did not manage to write a hit song right at the beginning of his musical career: but then, he did not grow up, as Ivor did, in an almost exclusively musical atmosphere.

He was born at Teddington, in Middlesex, in 1899, the son of a clerk who had married the daughter of a Naval officer. His father's family was enthusiastically musical, in an amateur way: his father and mother had met as members of the choir of St Alban's Church. His mother was a great theatre-goer, and took him with her as soon as he was old enough to enjoy himself; they queued together for the pit for most of the day in order to be sure of a seat in the front row at *A Waltz Dream*, *The Chocolate Soldier*, or *The Merry Widow*. *The Quaker Girl*, too, was one of his favourites – mainly perhaps because he had a memorable 'crush' on its star, Gertie Millar.

That he had an intensely good and accurate musical ear was demonstrated when he was still a child: he could come home after a visit to a new musical comedy and play a good deal of the score on the piano, getting both melodies and harmonies right, from memory. He was also singing and accompanying himself from the age of seven (his first success was a busy rendition of 'Coo', from *The Country Girl*, at a school concert), and it is recorded that he performed a 'Song and Dance' at a St Alban's Church bazaar when he was not much older. Sent to a Dancing Academy in Hanover Square, he stepped onto the professional stage for the first time when he was ten, in *The Goldfish*, 'A Fairy Play in Three Acts'. There had never been much doubt that the only thing he ever really wanted to do was perform; and after his first appearance at the Little Theatre (the *Daily Graphic* said 'great success is scored by Master Noël Coward as Prince Mussel') there was certainly never to be any question about his career.

The following year, he went into a play called *The Great Name*, at the Prince of Wales Theatre. The star was Charles Hawtrey, the brilliant light comedy actor. Coward worried Hawtrey's life out with technical enquiries about the playing of this or that line, this or that piece of business; ever afterwards he paid great tribute to what he had learned from that master of comedy. He already had a deep interest in the technique of acting and playwriting which was to result in his becoming one of the most consummate comedy actors of his own generation, and an admirable craftsman as a maker of plays.

His theatrical career continued without too many setbacks: it was of course far easier to make a living as an actor in the first years of the century than it is today – there were, then, many provincial theatres as well as those in London. Not that Coward saw many of them: he played Slightly in *Peter Pan* in the West End when he was fifteen; appeared in that famous Christmas play *Where the Rainbow Ends*; went into various plays for children.

His earliest interests as a writer for the theatre centred on songs and lyrics. 'Forbidden Fruit' had seemed to come so easily that from that moment on he was always writing songs. When he was seventeen, a friend, the composer Max Darewski, with whom he had been collaborating, managed to procure for him a contract with his brother's music-publishing company. None of the lyrics he wrote for the firm during the first year of the three-year contract impressed Darewski's – but he nevertheless received his cheque for £50. The second year, this became £75. By that time Coward had ceased to bother even to submit lyrics; and the £100 he received from the firm for the third year's inactivity only just came through before Darewski's went bankrupt.

Another firm did, however, accept one song which he had written with a Miss Doris Joel – 'The Baseball Rag':

> It's a joy, it's a dream,
> It's a yell, it's a scream,
> Oh, that Baseball Rag!

Writing the lyrics for other people's tunes did not greatly appeal, however, and it was only the fact that no-one seemed to like his own tunes much that drove Coward to do it. And when he was nineteen, the sale of his first play *The Last Trick* (for $500, to America) persuaded him to turn his

Noël Coward in 1930.

attention, for the time, wholly to writing. He wrote *I'll Leave It to You*, which was produced at the New Theatre in 1920, with Coward in the cast. Though it only ran for thirty-seven performances, it placed his name before the public, and received good reviews, leading to productions of *The Rat Trap*, *The Young Idea*, *Sirocco*, *Easy Virtue*, *The Queen was in the Parlour*, *Fallen Angels*, and the smash hit, *The Vortex* – all within five years!

It was with *The Vortex*, in 1924, that Coward became a celebrity. The play dealt with a young man of advanced sexual *mores* and his mother who took drugs; it glanced sideways at incest, and was at the time extremely shocking. Coward was 'taken up' by the society magazines, and when one photographer called on him in the relatively early morning, Coward received him sitting up in bed clad in a silk dressing-gown. In the resulting portrait, his eyes half-closed against the flash-bulb's explosion, he looked, as he later said, 'like an elderly Chinese manderin'. From that moment, silk dressing-gowns and a rather weary look were 'in'.

Followed about town by fashion reporters and gossip-writers, Coward joined the small band of men who set a fashion: not only for dressing-gowns but for polo-necked sweaters. The illustrated papers of the time are full of photographs of him – usually at some party or another, and usually (to judge by the expressions of his companions) saying something 'amusing'. For Coward, a much more intelligent man than his rival Ivor Novello, the glamour soon wore off, and the whole situation became rather trying.

Perhaps fortunately for him, he never became a public idol, as Ivor did: for one thing, he was not nearly as handsome – though his face had considerable character, and he used it expressively. For another, he saw himself as a serious writer and performer, and consequently often appeared in plays and wrote plays which the general public found, if amusing, rather too unconventional for its comfort. And finally, his homosexuality expressed itself in a sharper wit, a more pointedly feline style, than Ivor's, so that even those members of the public disposed to admire him uncritically were perhaps thrown a little off-balance by a quality which, though inexpressible, was somewhat worrying.

His large output in the early twenties did not swamp Coward's musical talent. André Charlot was at first unimpressed by Coward: 'Kindly do not waste my time with people like that ever again!' he had snapped in 1917, when Beatrice Lillie brought the young man to play and sing to him. But later he listened to some of Coward's numbers, and thought sufficiently well of them to engage him to prepare a whole revue. *London Calling* opened at the Duke of York's in 1923 with Coward and Gertrude Lawrence, and ran for 316 performances, after splendid reviews. For the first, but not the last time critics marvelled at Coward's versatility. *The Times* wrote:

> Mr Noël Coward is the Pooh-Bah of this production. He takes a leading part in it, and acts, dances and sings with credit; he helped Mr Ronald Jeans to write the 'book', and

also wrote the lyrics and music. To him, therefore, the greatest praise is due, for it was his handiwork that gave the others many of their opportunities of shining.

The one number to survive from *London Calling* is 'Parisian Pierrot', which Gertrude Lawrence sang. But the show was important in one particular way: it was the first time Elsie April was associated with Coward. Unable to write down a note of music, he relied on her to transcribe all his songs – she did this from 1923 until the beginning of the Second World War. He was the first to acknowledge an enormous debt to her, as well as to his various orchestrators.

More plays – *Hay Fever, This Was a Man, The Marquise,* and *Home Chat* – were produced before Coward turned to his first operetta, *Bitter Sweet*. So were more revues – now for Charles B. Cochran. *On with the Dance* opened at the London Pavilion in 1925 with Douglas Byng, Hermione Baddeley, Ernest Thesiger and Alice Delysia. It played for 229 performances. From the score came 'Poor Little Rich Girl', which alone is remembered.

In 1928, *This Year of Grace* opened, again at the London Pavilion, and again for Cochran. Douglas Byng was once more in the cast, with Sonnie Hale (who sang 'Dance, Little Lady' and, with Jessie Matthews, 'A Room with a View').

Bitter Sweet came next – that extraordinary success which remains the highpoint of Coward's career as a writer for the musical stage. Then another success, *Private Lives* (with Gertrude Lawrence playing opposite Coward in an unforgettable duet); and an even greater one, *Cavalcade* – an extraordinary pageant of English life between 1899 and 1931 (a period exactly corresponding to Coward's own life) which made use of elaborate scenes such as the departure of a troop-ship for the Boer War, a seaside promenade complete with bandstand, a train steaming out of a station with men for the Western Front, and Armistice Night in Trafalgar Square. It had several memorable theatrical moments – as when a family watched Queen Victoria's funeral procession from a window, and a small boy, turning away after standing at attention as the coffin passed, said: 'She must have been a very *little* lady'; or when a honeymoon couple had a scene standing on the deck of a liner, and moved away at the end of the scene to reveal a lifebuoy bearing the name SS *Titanic*, as the orchestra softly played 'Abide with Me'.

Though *Cavalcade* was not strictly a musical, Coward made brilliant use of the popular songs of the century, and wrote for the play some excellent numbers of his own. There was, for instance, a play-within-a-play – the production of a musical comedy, *Mirabelle* – for which he wrote a waltz-song, 'Lover of my Dreams', a comedy number, 'Fun on the Farm', and a finale (which was interrupted by the news that Mafeking had been relieved!) Then there was 'Twentieth Century Blues', sung in a night-club towards the end of the show, and leading to the splendidly theatrical final curtain – much more like the finale of a musical than of a play: spotlights lit several small scenes one after the other – a group of incurably wounded men from the First World War sat making baskets; the main characters from the piece danced, listened to the radio, played the piano, drank . . . In the words of Coward's own stage-direction:

> The visions are repeated quicker and quicker, while across the darkness runs a Riley light sign spelling out news. Noise grows louder and louder. Steam rivets, loudspeakers, jazz bands, aeroplane propellors, etc., until the general effect is complete chaos. Suddenly it all fades into darkness and silence and away at the back a Union Jack glows through the darkness.

And *Cavalcade* ended with the whole company singing 'God Save the King'.

After this bravura piece, Coward turned again to revue, and for *Words and Music* (1932) wrote 'Mad Dogs and Englishmen', 'Mad About the Boy' and several other numbers, including 'The Party's Over Now', with which, years later, he almost invariably ended his cabaret performances. After *Design for Living* (1933), came his second 'musical' – he called it 'a romantic comedy with music' – *Conversation Piece*. This was inspired by a casual reading of a Regency novel, while Coward was cruising in the Caribbean in HMS *Dragon*, as the guest of the Navy. He composed the play as a vehicle for the French star Yvonne Printemps, who though she had appeared in London in drama, had never done so in *operette*, the *genre* for which she was famous in Paris. For her, he wrote one of his most bewitching numbers, 'I'll Follow my Secret Heart'. There was also a charming number, little-remembered but extremely engaging, 'Nevermore'. But the rest of the score – which included 'There's Always Something Fishy about the French' – was less than his best.

The scene of *Conversation Piece* is set in Regency Brighton, where the Duc de Chaucigny-Varennes (played, in a highly suspicious French accent, by Coward) has established Melanie (Yvonne Printemps) as a refugee aristocrat who, he hopes, will make a good marriage, thus ensuring an income for both of them. Melanie, in reality an ex-acrobat the Duc had found in a café, is wooed by the Marquis of Sheere, whose parents offer her £1000 to leave England immediately. Sheer's father also offers her his own 'protection'. But she rejects both propositions, and those of other would-be lovers, including the Prince Regent ('Handsome though your Prince may be,/He is far too broad in the beam for me', she sings). She is, of course, in love with the Duc, and despite the fact that they both pretend that their affections lie elsewhere, they are united at the final curtain.

The first night of *Conversation Piece*, February 16, 1934, was eagerly awaited – it was looked upon as the successor to *Bitter Sweet*. There were long queues at the theatre, and tickets were exchanged at black-market prices. At the final curtain, the applause was so enthusiastic that Yvonne

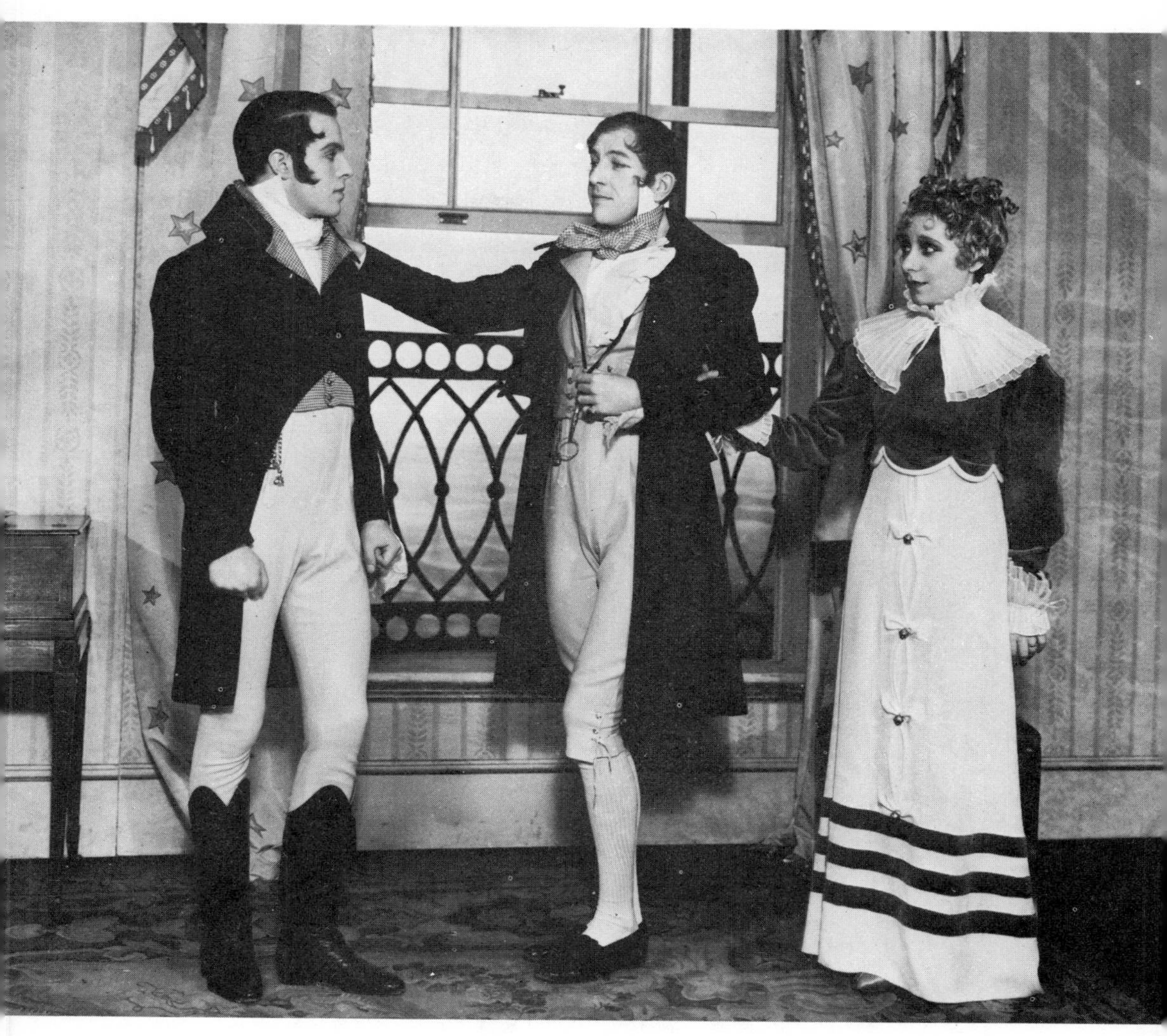

M. le Duc de Chaucigny-Varennes (Noël Coward) patronises the Marquis of Sheere (Louis Hayward) while the delectable Melanie (Yvonne Printemps) looks on. *Conversation Piece* (1934) was specially written for Printemps, who was reduced to tears by the ovation she received on the first night. 'I'll Follow my Secret Heart' was the best number of Coward's score.

Printemps was reduced to tears. She had been, indeed, delightful as Melanie: 'She is . . . an exquisite actress, with a bewitching personality', wrote W. A. Darlington in *The Daily Telegraph*. 'She sings, too, with the unfettered ease of a bird. It was from the moment when she first sang the romantic theme-song "I'll Follow my Secret Heart" (of which we shall hear more anon from all the gramophones in the world) that she had her audience in thrall.'

She must have been greatly relieved, for she had no English, and had learned the part parrot-fashion (when one listens to the dialogue on the original cast recordings of the piece, her accent sounds even more phoney than Coward's!) There was some difficulty with her during the show's run of 177 performances: she was easily bored, and would often pretend that her voice had gone. One night she had been singing in a mere croak when Coward pointed out the figure of the great violinist Fritz Kreisler sitting at his invitation in the wings. 'Mon Dieu, c'est Kreeslair!' she cried, and sang superbly for the rest of the evening. 'Better get Tauber for tomorrow night', dryly remarked another member of the cast.

With *Point Valaine*, a failure, and the brilliant success of his two evenings of one-act plays, *Tonight at 8.30*, intervening, Coward's next musical was *Operette*, produced at His Majesty's in 1938. It ran for only 133 performances, and must be counted a relative failure, despite the fact that it contains the show-stopping 'Stately Homes of England', the nostalgic 'Where are the Songs we Sung?', and the lovely waltz-song 'Dearest Love'.

Coward had attempted another direct follow-up to *Bitter Sweet*. The show was written for Peggy Wood, and for the Viennese singer Fritzi Massary, who came out of retirement to play in it. The story concerns a Gaiety Girl, Rozanne Gray (Peggy Wood), with whom Lord Vaynham (Griffith Jones) falls in love. They become lovers, but she refuses to marry him partly because it would interfere with her ambition to become a star, and partly because of his parents' opposition. She does indeed become a star – but also succumbs to Nigel Vaynham's pleas, and agrees to marry him. Though deeply in love, and prepared to sacrifice her career for him, she gives him up when his mother points out that marriage to an actress would ruin his Army career.

The story is fustian, which does not matter in the least, but Coward fudged it – remarkably, for so clever a maker of plays. There were several good dramatic moments, but they were contrived; the sub-plot involving Fritzy Massary (as the operetta star Liesl Haren) is unclear and disconnected, and despite the cleverly-managed show-within-a-show, *The Model Maid*, an excellent pastiche of a dated musical comedy, the action flagged. The notices were on the whole bad. The kindest was Ivor Brown's in *The Sketch*, where he commended the music as 'sweet and soothing and wholly suitable. It contributes to an entertainment as far removed as possible from the world of jazz and jitters.'

Coward, later, was to argue that *Operette* was the least successful of his musical plays; he thought the music was 'meagre and only at moments adequate' (which is perhaps over-critical), and justly pointed out that the plot established 'triumphant confusion' in the minds of the audience by switching to and fro between the stage play and the real play. 'I remember peering from my box at the Opera House, Manchester [at the try-out] and watching bewildered playgoers rustling their programmes and furtively striking matches in a frantic effort to discover where they were and what was going on.'

Present Laughter, *Blithe Spirit* and *This Happy Breed* occupied the war years, together, of course, with much other activity; and it was not until 1946 that his next musical was seen in London. Called *Pacific 1860*, it re-opened the Theatre Royal, Drury Lane, after the war. *Pacific 1860* had been planned for His Majesty's, and went into the much larger Drury Lane theatre not (as has been supposed) because anyone especially thought that a Coward musical would be just the thing to re-open that theatre after its wartime closure (it had been the headquarters of ENSA, and had also been damaged by bombing), but simply because His Majesty's was not available, and it was calculated that the Lane could be repaired and made ready in time.

From the beginning, things went wrong. A permit to repair the bomb damage was refused, and only special pleading from Coward resulted in a last-minute reversal of the decision; so that instead of the week or ten days of dress rehearsal which Coward had specifically required, there were only two – and the seating was only replaced in the theatre three days before the opening night. There could be no out-of-town try-out because it was the middle of the pantomime season, and no theatres were available. Then there was the problem of heating Drury Lane. The central heating system failed to work after six years of disuse, and rehearsals and performances took place in an almost zero temperature. Finally, Mary Martin, the American singer, who was to make a great hit a few years later at Drury Lane in *South Pacific*, was badly miscast in a very English romantic musical in which she was supposed to appear as an ultra-sophisticated woman of the world, full of wit and charm and worldly wisdom.

Miss Martin played Elena Salvador, an opera star recovering from an illness on the South Pacific island of Samolo (an island Coward had invented some years previously, and for which he made up a complete history, together with a language which could actually be learned and spoken – and it was in the play). Elena meets and falls in love with Kerry (Graham Payn), the son of a planter; and he loves her. But the romance is unthinkable, for Elena is regarded by the British colonists as extremely fast, having been seen riding in breeches. So Elena leaves the island and Kerry, to return two years later just in time for the celebration of a wedding – which turns out not to be Kerry's wedding, as she at first supposes, but his brother's; so the couple are united happily just as the curtain falls.

The play cannot be said to be one of Coward's most convincing, though it has the carefully engineered climaxes at which he was so good – as when, at the end of Act II scene i, at a party at the planter's house to which Kerry has invited Elena without his parents' permission, they dance a polka together to the scandal of the guests. At the end of the dance:

Suddenly, as though impelled by some force over which she has no control, Elena leans forward and kisses [Kerry] on the mouth. There is a gasp from everybody and then an ominous silence. Elena, realising that she has gone much too far, pulls herself together, curtsies low to the Stirlings and Their Excellencies, bows to every-one else, and, summoning Rosa and Felix with an imperious wave of her hand, goes up the steps. The guests part to enable her to get through. The silence continues. It is not until the crack of her coachman's whip and the jingle of her carriage bells is heard, that the whispering starts. It grows and grows until everyone on the stage is talking at once. The curtain falls.

The lyrics of *Pacific 1860* are deft and, as usual, admirably twinned to the book. Only with the number, in which a double sextet of the Governor's ADCs explain to the ladies the nature of their duties, is Coward at his absolute best in that department:

> Every minute we're made to sin it is really very
> depraved;
> But to Hell with the lies we tell – His Excellency's
> honour must be saved.
>
> His Excellency regrets
> That owing to an attack of gout he really cannot
> venture out on Saturday to dine.
> His Excellency regrets
> That owing to doctor's orders he cannot attend the
> Mission tea and also must decline
> Your kind invitation
> For Wednesday week.
> A slight operation
> And poor circulation
> Combined with a weedy physique
> Has made him unable to speak –
> All this in addition to what
> The doctors describe as a 'clot'
> Which may disappear by the end of the year but may,
> very possibly, not!
> His Excellency regrets
> That owing to his exalted state he can no more associate
> with amiable brunettes.
> Walk up, walk up, we're willing to take your bets
> That that's one of the principal things
> His Excellency regrets.

In the end, as Coward said when introducing the printed text of *Pacific 1860* in his *Play Parade*, what really mattered was the score. He wrote it as an attempt to recapture the charm which seemed to him by then to have deserted the musical play, and thought it 'one of the best things I have ever done'. The public thought otherwise. 'This is a Changing World', in which Elena's companion, Rosa, warns her against the unwisdom of her new romance, has considerable charm, and several of the numbers have the Coward wit running through them, but by 1946, they seemed somewhat dated – and, worse, simply the mixture as before, but not as efficacious. 'I

Wish I wasn't Quite such a Big Girl', for instance, a number for a plump teenager, fell flat.

In 1950, *Ace of Clubs* was produced at the Cambridge, and though it ran for 211 performances, rather demonstrated again that Coward had been left behind by the latest American development of the musical play. He attempted to make it more 'contemporary' by peopling the stage with gangsters, black-marketeers, and tough chorus-girls, and by a plot in which the love of a handsome young sailor (Graham Payn) for the star of a somewhat sleazy night-club floor show, Pinkie Leroy (Pat Kirkwood) is obstructed by a complicated plot concerning a parcel of stolen jewellery.

The notices were mixed. Coward, for a number of reasons, most of them silly, had lost much of his popularity with the critics and indeed the public. He was even booed at the first night. Alan Dent, one of the kinder critics, wrote in the *News Chronicle* 'It is not the ace of trumps, but it will serve to take a trick.' 'Sail Away', the lead romantic number, was good – Coward revived it years later as the title-song of another musical; there was a good popular number, 'Chase Me, Charlie', for Pat Kirkwood to sing in her persona as night-club star; and there was the by now obligatory comedy number, 'Three Juvenile Delinquents', which had the kind of success achieved by a similar number, 'Officer Krupke', in Leonard Bernstein's *West Side Story* in a few years' time.

Listening to the original cast recordings, it is difficult not to conclude that obvious and crude orchestration were at least partly responsible for the relative failure of some of the numbers. The charming 'Why Does Love Get in the Way?' was over-lushly orchestrated in a big-band style, while 'I Like America', delightfully sung by Graham Payn, is much more effective in a later recording made by Coward himself, with an altogether wittier orchestration. The same is true of 'Josephine', which was written for Pat Kirkwood. Altogether, *Ace of Clubs* was perhaps unlucky.

The age of the really outstanding Coward musical was now over. *After the Ball*, produced at the Globe in 1954, was an attempt to set Oscar Wilde's *Lady Windermere's Fan* to music. Not one number from the score is popularly remembered. Alone among the critics, Harold Hobson welcomed the show ecstatically. It ran for only 188 performances.

The return to popularity and a new peak of success for Noël Coward began with his spectacular performances in cabaret at the Café de Paris in 1951. *Nude With Violin*, *Waiting in the Wings*, and *Look After Lulu* (an adaptation of a Feydeau farce) had varying degrees of success, and he began to make occasional appearances on film. His only previous real success in that medium had been his own war film *In Which We Serve*. Now a late screen career began with a marvellous comedy performance in the film version of Graham Greene's *Our Man in Havana*.

In 1961, *Sail Away*, his first musical to have its premiere in New York, starred Elaine Stritch as Mimi Paragon, hostess on a cruise liner. Originally, the character at the centre of the show had been a certain Mrs Wentworth-Brewster, who, Coward fans will recall, achieved a certain notoriety as the result of her behaviour 'In a Bar on the Piccola Marina'. Once more, the score was not particularly memorable: the title-song came straight out of *Ace of Clubs*, and certainly deserved renewed attention, and there was one extremely amusing and apt number: 'Why Do the Wrong People Travel (while the right people stay at home)?'. 'Where Shall I Find Him?' and 'Something Very Strange' were two numbers in the true Coward romantic idiom.

Though the first night was a riotous success, the notices were somewhat indifferent, and the show folded after only six months – a pattern repeated almost identically when it was presented in London in June 1962.

During most of 1962, Coward worked on the music and lyrics for a musical version of Terence Rattigan's *The Sleeping Prince*, produced on Broadway the following year, re-titled *The Girl Who Came to Supper*. It was dogged by misfortune from the beginning: a song entitled 'Long Live the King – If He Can!' had to be cut hurriedly from the score when President Kennedy was assassinated, and replaced by a number from *Operette*; the try-outs were less than satisfactory; and when the show opened, critics found it dismal. Its one triumph was the appearance of the British music-hall comédienne Tessie O'Shea, who stopped the show every night with a medley of imitation Cockney knees-up songs. This was the only one of Coward's musicals never to be seen in Britain – and though the next, *High Spirits*, a musical version of *Blithe Spirit* with Beatrice Lillie as Madame Arcati, did marvellously well in New York, it ran only briefly in London, where Cecily Courtneidge took over Miss Lillie's role.

By this time, the Coward revival was thriving. While *High Spirits* was a relative failure in the West End, across the river at the Old Vic a National Theatre production (by the Master himself) of perhaps his best play, *Hay Fever* – in which Edith Evans made her last major stage appearance – was a sensation: one of the most joyous entertainments to be seen on the London stage during the sixties. Only a few weeks later, a revival of *Private Lives* transferred to the West End from the Hampstead Theatre Club, and ran to full houses. If his career as a writer of musical plays had rather spluttered out, he was certainly secure enough as a man of the theatre.

The Coward revival of the sixties, which culminated in a knighthood conferred on him in the 1970 honours list, may have been based to some extent on nostalgia. As the dramatist John Whiting said in the *London Magazine*: '*Sail Away* is the bluntest thing to have struck the West End theatre for many a year . . . but speaking as one twenty years his junior, all I can ask is: who doesn't love his youth? For that is what Coward is to men of my age: *Private Lives*, *Conversation Piece*, *Operette*, *Tonight at 8.30*, and all those songs we sang to our girls driving back in the red MG from the Thames pub on a summer night in 1936.'

But Coward's success in the *genre* of the musical play was more firmly based than that. His theatrical flair was considerable, his technique well-practised, his musical talent generous and ingenious. He was an admirable director of his own work, and when he appeared in it he always played to great effect. He took enormous care over the books of his musicals, highly conscious that it was unwise to depend (as Ivor Novello did) almost entirely on the music. His books and lyrics are witty, highly literate, and sufficiently sophisticated (though not, as some critics have alleged, to the point of caricature).

When he failed in construction, as for instance in *Operette*, it was in a sense because he tried to pack too much into a show; or, sometimes, because the insertion of a number which failed to have much to do with the surrounding plot weakened the line of the piece. This last failing became more notable as the years went by, and the new American musicals emphasised homogeneity of book and numbers. His often extremely amusing comedy numbers were almost all gratuitous: 'His Excellency Regrets' is not inapposite in *Pacific 1860*, nor 'Regency Rakes' in *Conversation Piece*; but 'Three Juvenile Delinquents' has not much to do with *Ace of Clubs*, nor 'The Stately Homes of England' with *Operette*. The period is right, but that is all.

As to his virtues as a composer: he was, like Ivor Novello, a musical illiterate. He could tinkle away on the piano in an attractive and useful way, but he could not write a note of music, and his attempts to learn something about technique were spasmodic and unsuccessful. He and Fred Astaire once signed on together for a course at the Guildhall School of Music, but Coward alleged that at the first lecture they were told that one Ebenezer Prout had forbidden the use of consecutive fifths many years ago, and that therefore they should never be employed. Remarking that if consecutive fifths were good enough for Debussy and Ravel, they were good enough for *him*, Coward left. That all sounds a little unlikely: Coward's post-script to the story is probably the truth – drawn as he was, not only to music but to drama and performance, there simply wasn't time to study musical theory. Fortunately, his excellent ear enabled him to be at home in sophisticated melody, and his inventiveness is a constant delight to the listener; the fact that he had an expert musical amanuensis in Elsie April, and often first-rate orchestrators was of course a boon.

There was no general rule about his methods of composition. Some scores came easier to him than others; but it seems that in general melodies tended to drop into his mind fairly readily. 'I'll See You 'Again' fell into his head, verse and chorus, when he was one day stuck in a New York traffic jam. The one problem was getting home so that he could play it on the piano and have it written down before he forgot it. On another occasion, when searching for a main theme for *Conversation Piece*, he finally gave up after ten days, switched off the lights in his workroom, and was about to go to bed when he noticed that the lamp on the piano was still burning. Ill-temperedly he walked over to switch it off, inexplicably sat down, and played 'I'll Follow my Secret Heart' straight through without a single hesitation.

There is nothing unique about that, of course; poets are used to being 'given' lines in a similar manner, and Siegfried Sassoon records the composition of *Everything Burst Out Singing* in precisely the same way. But of course it *is* puzzling. 'How can a theme come to me complete like that?' asked Coward; 'How can it be accounted for, and where does it come from?' There is no answer.

6

Ivor Novello

'If it is nonsense, it is glamorous nonsense . . . ' – THE DAILY TELEGRAPH

Ivor Novello was in the habit of making private recordings of the first nights of his musicals. One recalls Mary Ellis and Olive Gilbert giving the first public performance of 'The Wings of Sleep' from the 1939 first night of *The Dancing Years*. To listen to it is to recapture for a moment or two the atmosphere of a Novello first night: one can almost hear the anticipation of the audience as the cue-line for the number is spoken; the two voices rise and fall in a melodic line the charm of which is absolutely indisputable; then, as the number ends, comes a roar of applause which goes on and on until only a scene-change, and Novello himself pounding a piano to introduce the next dialogue, end it. Even in the days of his greatest success – between 1935, when *Glamorous Night* was produced, and his death in 1951 – he had his critics: those who found the incurably romantic plots cloying, and the music too charming by half. But Ivor Novello's musicals packed theatres from stalls to gods, and many of his songs continue to be sung and played.

Novello – known to his family, friends, colleagues and to his audiences simply as 'Ivor' – was a Welshman, born in 1893 in Cardiff. His father was a charming, handsome, insignificant civil servant, a rate-collector for the city council. His mother was the remarkable Madame Clara Novello Davies, teacher of singing and choir-mistress – who, when her son was only six months old, left him to go with her Welsh Ladies' Choir to the Chicago World's Fair.

'Mam', as Ivor always called her, was the daughter of two singers. Her father had encouraged her to form her own ladies' choir, and with it she had considerable financial as well as artistic success. She was determined that Ivor should be a musician as well as, of course, a perfect child. She was somewhat daunted when he proved to be an almost excessively ugly baby. But as to his musicality, there was no doubt: when he was very young, at a little private music school in Cathedral Road, Cardiff, he found it easy to carry a tune in a particularly pure soprano voice, and Mam was delighted.

Her personality no doubt contributed to the boy's addiction to theatricality – even before he became besotted by the theatre. She was *très grande-dame*, given to sweeping about Cardiff looking like an overdressed Christmas tree, covered with jewels and complimentary medals and orders she had gathered throughout her musical life. When she opened a London studio, she took Ivor with her on many of her visits there; and he began to go regularly to the theatre, and to enjoy it – overmuch, Mam felt, and bustled him away to school in Gloucester. During the short time he was there, she set about obtaining for him a scholarship to the Magdalen Choir School at Oxford. David Davies, the father, who had always disliked the idea of his son entering so precarious a career as music, went so far as to hide the application form. But in vain: in 1903, Ivor won the scholarship.

He seems to have enjoyed his time at Oxford, especially when set to sing solos in chapel. He did not enjoy his musical theory: Dr Herbert Brewer, organist of Gloucester Cathedral, with whom he studied harmony and counterpoint, remembered him as one of the laziest pupils he ever had. But he already 'wrote music', and when he was seventeen not only had a song, 'The Spring of the Year', published, but actually accompanied its performance at the Albert Hall. It was not a success.

For the whole of his life, at school and even more in the holidays, he did nothing but listen to – or at least, hear – music. He accompanied his mother's choir, he was present at their concerts and rehearsals; at home, he could hardly be in the house at any time when music was not sounding out from one room or another. It was not, of course, 'good' music – the songs in which his mother's pupils and to some extent her choir excelled were the salon music of the late Victorian age, and it might be claimed that this had its effect on his later compositions.

From Oxford, Ivor went home to Cardiff. But when not in Wales, he lived at his mother's flat in Bond Street, going more and more to the theatre – to plays, to the opera, but mainly to the Gaiety and Daly's. And he spent a great deal of his time writing songs: twenty-five of these were published by the time he was twenty-one, including 'The Little Damozel' (1912), still occasionally to be heard.

In 1912, Ivor went to New York. He had written some music for the Festival of Empire at the Crystal Palace, and went to Canada as part of a misconceived plan to export the show. From there he went to America, and while in New York composed and attempted to sell a complete musical comedy, *The Fickle Jade*. The idea had been sprung by a competition organised by Chappell & Co., the music publishers. The *Evening Standard*, in an account of one of Mam's concerts, spoke of her son as being in America for 'the production of his new opera'. One can almost hear Mam referring to *The Fickle Jade* as 'an opera'! But it was never to be performed, though some of its music was heard in later Novello shows: 'The Skating Waltz' in *Glamorous Night* (1935) came from the earlier score.

The outbreak of the First World War brought Ivor his first and in some ways most enduring success. By 1914, he and Mam were living in a flat above the Strand Theatre in the Aldwych – where he was to die thirty-seven years later. He was not at all enthusiastic about the war, or the fact that he might well be forced to play a part in it. On the face of it, he was an extremely unlikely man to write a good war song – and it seems, indeed, that Mam forced him into it by writing an execrable one herself, and threatening to perform it in public.

'Keep the Home Fires Burning' was composed, like most of Ivor's songs, very quickly indeed. He wrote some of the words, and the rest of the lyric was completed by an American friend, Lena Guilbert Ford, later killed in an air raid. It was first sung during a concert at the Alhambra organised by the National Sunday League (formed in an attempt to liven up the deadly dullness of the English Sunday). Ivor accompanied one of Mam's pupils, Sybil Vane; and the occasion was very different to that of four years' earlier, when a shallow patter of applause had greeted his florid waltz-song 'The Spring of the Year'. As Miss Vane repeated the chorus of 'Till the Boys Come Home' (as the song was first called), she and Ivor heard a low humming from the audience, almost as though it was joining in. When the chorus came a third time, the hum became a positive song. The number had to be repeated again and again; even the Guards Band, on the platform behind the singer, vamped an accompaniment.

Ivor, like Byron, woke up next morning to find himself famous. And 'Keep the Home Fires Burning', becoming the best-known song of the First World War, earned £15,000 during the first five years of its life. It became popular again during the Second World War, and was even regularly performed in the years between – though sometimes in rather odd forms, as when the Unionist Party, during the 1923 election, took the tune and added its own words:

> Stand for home and neighbour,
> Spurn all foreign labour,
> Baldwin's way's the British Way
> And it's bound to pay.

And in 1931 Mam herself presented 'Keep the PEACE Fires Burning' as the theme song of her Women's League of Peace.

In 1916, Ivor joined the Royal Naval Air Service. A catastrophically bad pilot, he was grounded and given clerical work at the Air Ministry, where he spent at least some of his time at work on music for the first musical comedy of which he wrote a substantial part: *Theodore and Co.*, produced at the Gaiety in 1916. George Grossmith and H. M. Harwood had adapted *Theodore and Co.* from a farce by the French writer Pierre Gavault, and Jerome Kern had agreed to write the music. But in the end, thirteen numbers were contributed by Ivor. Two of them are as catchy as anything written at that time: 'What a Duke Should Be' and 'Every Little Girl Can Teach Me Something New' derived directly from the musicals which Ivor had been hearing at the Gaiety for the past ten years.

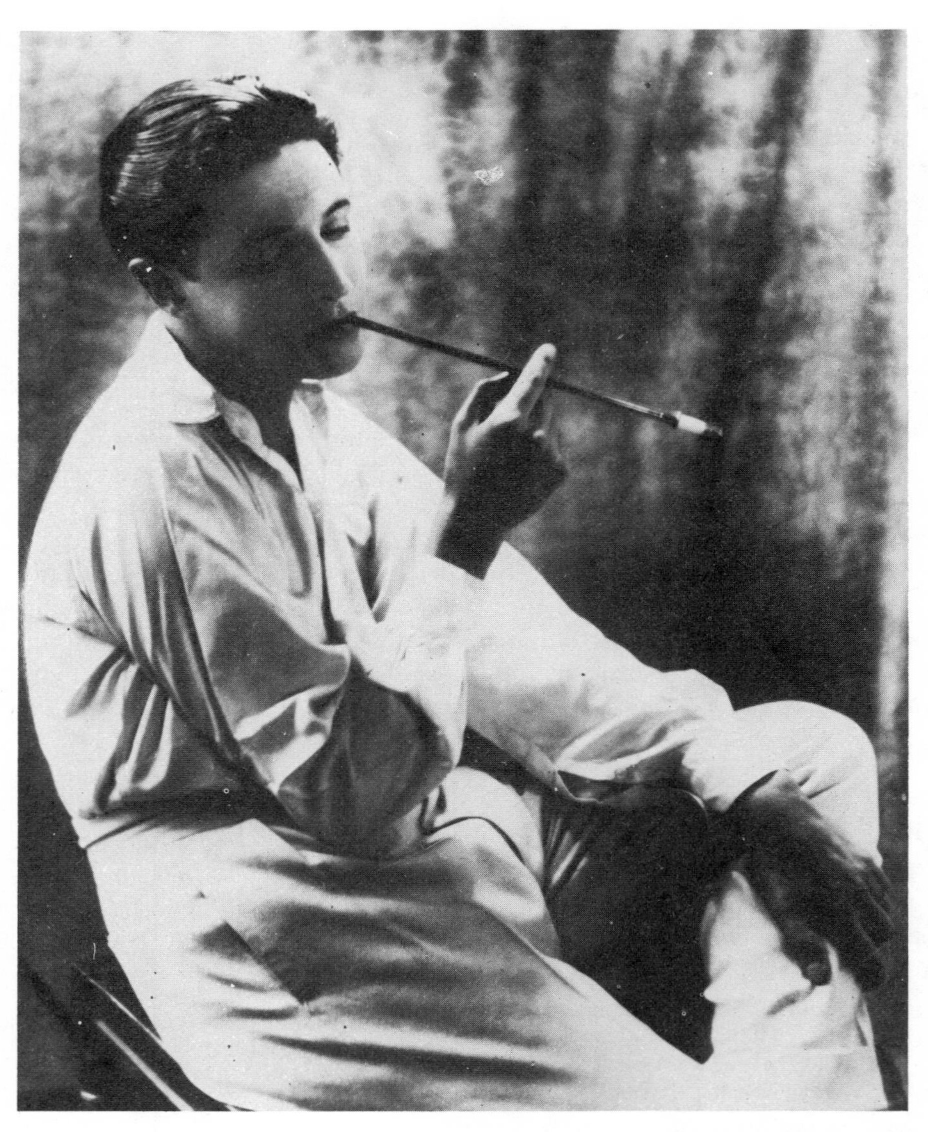

Ivor Novello in the late '20s – the vastly successful, vastly popular film-star, stage actor, composer and playwright in a pose which now looks suspiciously satirical, but at the time was the height of chic.

Theodore & Co. had a good run: 'it seems to be on for the duration', wrote the *Sunday Herald*. An excellent cast was headed by George Grossmith (until his enlistment), and Leslie Henson and Davy Burnaby also took part. A little later, at the Shaftesbury, Grossmith co-produced *Arlette*, a vehicle for the popular star Joseph Coyne – though it was Stanley Lupino who had the 'smash hit' number, 'I'm on the Staff', one of the seven songs contributed to the score by Ivor. 'The People's King', the first of a long list of tributes to the conception of monarchy, was another.

It was 1921 before Ivor was entrusted with the entire score of a musical comedy. In the meantime he had written eleven songs for *Who's Hooper?* (presented at the Adelphi in 1919). The show was based on Pinero's farce *In Chancery*, and starred W. H. Berry; during its run of 349 performances Ivor was presented to King George V, who had been an admirer of 'Keep the Home Fires Burning', and was to become a considerable fan of its composer. In 1920, Ivor wrote two numbers for *A Southern Maid*, an ill-fated successor to the popular *Maid of the Mountains*.

This was the period during which Ivor was moving into the twentieth century. His natural predilection had always been for the operettas of the Gaiety and Daly's. But this was now the age of Gershwin and *Lady be Good*, of Youmans and *No, No, Nanette!* For the moment, Ruritania, together with the world of romantic novelists such as Anthony Hope and Stanley Weyman, was out of fashion. By 1921, Ivor had realised this.

He had also, incidentally, made his first two films. The first was *The Call of the Blood* (1920), in which he played a young English husband killed by the father of the Sicilian girl whom he had seduced. His performance was much admired by Sarah Bernhardt, and before its release he had started work on his second film, *Miarka, Daughter of the Bear*, in which he appeared with no less an actress than the great Réjane (it was her last performance). It was an auspicious beginning to a film career which was to span fewer than fifteen years, but was to encompass twenty-three pictures, including the famous *The Rat* and Alfred Hitchcock's first film, *The Lodger*.

The Golden Moth (1921), with an original book by Fred Thompson and P. G. Wodehouse (for which the latter also wrote many of the lyrics) was Novello's first one-man musical comedy. The Golden Moth itself was a night-club, and most of the cast were gangsters – led by Dipper Tigg, played by W. H. Berry, for whom Novello wrote 'Dartmoor Days', a splendid number with an extremely catching tune. 'Give Me a Thought Now and Then' was another popular number. The show had only a moderate success: it ran for 281 performances.

For the next few years, Ivor concentrated on numbers for revue – though he contributed three songs to *Our Nell*, produced in 1924 at the Gaiety for José Collins. Most of the musical score was by Harold Fraser-Simpson, but Ivor wrote 'The Land of Might Have Been', perhaps the best song in the piece. The lyricist was 'Edward Moore' – a pseudonym which concealed the identity of Ivor's great friend Eddie Marsh, Winston Churchill's secretary, and one of the most discerning art patrons of his time. It was in *Our Nell*, too, that Ivor's stirring march song 'Our England' was first heard. It had been written years earlier, an attempt at a war song. Now, military bands threw themsleves at it with enthusiasm, and the British Fascists asked permission to use it as their official anthem.

In 1924, Ivor had his first triumph as a stage actor, in his own play (written with Constance Collier), *The Rat*. By the end of the twenties he was a matinée idol in the classic sense of the term – and also, by then, a highly successful playwright, with *The Truth Game* and *Symphony in Two Flats* to his credit. In the thirties were to come *I Lived with You*, *Fresh Fields*, *Proscenium*, *Murder in Mayfair*, and *Full House*.

As an actor, he rarely extended himself – and not only for selfish reasons. He had the disadvantage of having collected a band of fans who demanded his appearance always in the same kind of role: when he played Lord George Hell in an adaptation of Max Beerbohm's *The Happy Hypocrite* (at His Majesty's in 1936), the production failed because for much of the evening he was made up as an extremely ugly man. The public would not accept it – despite the fact that the critics expressed admiration for his performance.

It is an open question whether it was not an even greater disadvantage that he was extremely, almost excessively, handsome. His looks were not of the type that would be fashionable in the seventies: his was a perfect profile, without the slightest trace of any roughness to give it character. It was perhaps indeed a trifle weak, in repose, though when it was animated in a rewardingly dashing role on-stage it became a little more than conventionally handsome. The photographs of Ivor as Henry V, which he played in a production by Lewis Casson at Drury Lane at the time of the outbreak of the Second World War, show him as the very model of romantic royalty.

Undoubtedly, he was a trifle narcissistic. Rumour had it that the piano in his flat was surrounded by mirrors, so that when at the keyboard he could see himself from several angles. A passive homosexual, he was careful to preserve his figure (at every excuse, in the country, he would strip to a minimum of clothes to sunbathe) and as far as possible, his face. Towards the end of his life, he aged with a kind of noble weariness; the stills from his last show, *King's Rhapsody*, show greater character in his features than the photographs taken when he was 'the handsomest man in England' – because of the imperfections time had stamped there.

During the twenties and early thirties, his looks and his increasing experience as a film actor brought a stream of offers from producers; he concentrated on his acting, and restricted his composition to a few numbers only. He supplied various revues with some lively pieces – some of them extremely successful: 'And Her Mother Came Too', sung in *A to Z* by Jack Buchanan, was one of the most popular revue numbers of its time, and remained familiar until very recently. He also turned out some excellent numbers which have been more or less forgotten – like 'The Dowager Fairy Queen', written with Douglas Furber for Jack Hulbert's revue *The House That Jack Built* (1929). That was for Cecily Courtneidge, who also had the distinction of singing, on the halls, Ivor's 'And the Little Dog's Tail Went Up', a slightly naughty number which was banned by the Birmingham Watch Committee on the grounds of obscenity.

Ivor had, indeed, a sense of humour which could become rather endearingly ribald. He invented, for instance, distorted titles for his musicals (*The Prancing Queers*, *Perchance to Scream*, *Careless Rupture*), which might not have appealed to the romantics who crowded to see them. It is a little ironical, too, that the crowds of ladies who collected at the stage-doors in the hope of perhaps touching his shoulder as he passed by, should not have been aware that he was homosexual. But of course it did not matter.

It was in 1934 that Ivor suddenly conceived the idea of writing a musical for Drury Lane. W. Macqueen Pope, who is often inaccurate in detail, but whose theatre gossip usually had some foundation in fact, says in his rambling biography of Ivor that it was during a lunch at the Ivy with H. M. Tennent, then general manager of the Lane, that the notion came into Ivor's head. Drury Lane was at that time 'dark', and Tennent had been unable to discover a show which he was confident would succeed there – even at that time, mounting a musical which would fill that large stage satisfactorily was an expensive business, and there had to be a real chance of success before backers could be convinced.

Ivor suddenly asked Tennent why, instead of looking towards America, he had not asked *him*. 'I've got an idea for a show', he said – not in reality having anything of the sort. On the spot, he made up a story which indeed bore some resemblance to the final story-line of *Glamorous Night*. Tennent was impressed, and asked to see a full synopsis of the piece, which he could put before his board the following day. Within twenty-four hours Ivor produced the synopsis – and the board not only liked it, but agreed that Ivor should produce the entire show himself.

He telephoned Mary Ellis, the original star of *Rose Marie* in America, and announced that he hoped she would appear in his new Drury Lane musical: he had written 'some wonderful numbers' for her. (He had in fact not at that time written a single note of music; but by the time she came for tea next day, he had six numbers to play her.) She agreed to appear. He chose Oliver Messel as his designer, and Leontine Sagan, who had studied under Reinhardt, as his producer. For the lyrics he went to a young actor he had befriended, Christopher Hassall.

The cast was chosen with care. Ivor himself, of course, was to be at its centre. Mary Ellis, Lyn Harding, Elisabeth Welch, Barry Jones, Trefor Jones, Peter Graves and Olive Gilbert supported him. Many of them were to appear in every Novello musical until his last. As to the chorus, Ivor was incurably kind to them. Time and again, it is said, he would regard some old duck waddling down to the footlights at an audition, and would say: 'Oh, no – really, not again; she's past it!' Yet when the first night came, there she would be, singing lustily away in the back row.

Ivor's experience as actor and writer had prepared him well for the success of *Glamorous Night*. He had always been an incurable romantic – as the critics

Ivor Novello and Mary Ellis plight their troth at the gypsy wedding in *Glamorous Night* (1935).

never tired of telling him. He had written parts for himself as a destitute Russian prince (in *I Lived With You*), as a struggling young composer facing blindness (in *Symphony in Two Flats*), and as a handsome but penniless young adventurer (in *The Truth Game*). Now, he was to be a young inventor saving the King of Krasnia from assassination, and having a desperate affair with the King's mistress, a gypsy beauty who leaves him to become queen, and to be crowned during a ceremony which the inventor watches by means of his own invention – television!

The piece has everything. It has an extract from an opera (in which the gypsy, also a prima donna, performs on a stage-within-a-stage); it has an attempted assassination on stage, with a carriage drawn by a real horse; it has a romantic gypsy wedding scene; it has a court scene in which Ivor, in ordinary day-dress, walked down the length of the Drury Lane stage through a crowd of magnificently dressed courtiers, to pay his farewell to Krasnia; and it has the famous shipwreck scene, in which on the first night the audience was thrilled to see three decks of a cruise liner (in which the hero had taken refuge with his gypsy love) tilt and begin to sink, as sirens wailed, fog-horns blared, and smoke hid a panicking crowd of extras.

And quite apart from all that, there is the score – which remains one of Ivor's best. There is a soldiers chorus, 'Her Majesty Militza'; a blues, magnificently sung by Elisabeth Welch, whose part, nothing whatsoever to do with the plot, was put in just for that purpose! – justifiably, for she stopped the show with 'Far Away in Shanty-Town'. Mary Ellis sang 'Glamorous Night', the title-song, Mary Ellis and Trefor Jones the beautiful waltz-song 'Fold Your Wings'. Jones, a splendid tenor with operatic experience, turned a ringing tone to 'Shine Through My Dreams', one of the show's most popular songs.

Ivor's own popularity as a performer was probably at its apogee. Even ten years earlier there was almost a riot when he washed his legs in the first act of his excruciating melodrama, *Downhill*: 'His knees, his shins, even his thighs, and his dear little wiggly toes!' wrote St John Ervine in *The Observer*; 'If there were palpitations in the pit, there were signs of satisfaction in the gallery.' Now, his first entrance in *Glamorous Night* was greeted by an enormous roar of welcome, and by the time the evening ended it was clear that, whatever the Press said, the musical was a triumph.

And the Press was, in fact, kind. Ivor was never very popular with the professional critics (though most of them grudgingly recognised his growing power as an actor of a certain sort). But they approved of *Glamorous Night*, if with reservations. 'Wildly, inspiringly, intoxicatingly triumphant', said the *Daily Mail*; 'inspired punk, and it is given to few to write it', admitted the *Bystander*. *The Daily Telegraph* called Ivor 'a superb theatrical craftsman', and pointed out that 'if it is nonsense, it is glamorous nonsense, and for those who are ready to be entertained, it is the best show of its kind that Drury Lane has had for years'.

With hindsight, the behaviour of Drury Lane's management at this point seems almost incredible. There was a long-standing tradition that there was always pantomime at that theatre at Christmas; but Novello was none-the-less staggered to hear from the directors – after he had saved the theatre from probable bankruptcy – that after a run of only six months, *Glamorous Night* was to be taken off in favour of *Jack and the Beanstalk*. Business was good, and getting better, and there was no reason to suppose that the musical could not have enjoyed a very much longer run. Ivor went so far as to offer Drury Lane's board a guarantee of £8000 (what they might be expected to make from the pantomime production) if they would keep his show on. The board demanded £10,000 – which (even though *Glamorous*

Night had earned back its £25,000 production costs and was now making money) was impossible for him.

That was one disappointment. An even greater one lay ahead: there had been an unwritten agreement that Ivor was to prepare a second show for the Lane, and by the time *Glamorous Night* was into its short run, he had completed the book and score of *Careless Rapture*. He read the story and played the music to the board of the theatre, which at that time consisted almost entirely of businessmen rather than theatricals. Their reception was cold, and the news came very promptly that they did not approve of *Careless Rapture*.

They were to change their tune fairly rapidly. After the pantomime, the Lane mounted *Rise and Shine*, a musical by Harry Graham and Desmond Carter. It ran for only forty-four performances, and there was no show available to replace it. Approached by the board, Ivor understandably put his foot down. He would produce *Careless Rapture* there – but *he* would pay 75% of the production costs, and would take a proportionate profit.

Careless Rapture ran for ten months – but its success depended much more on the personality of its star and composer, and on the glamour and ingenuity of its elaborate set-pieces, than on the music or plot. It was written with Dorothy Dickson in mind. She played a musical-comedy star, about to retire and marry a rich man, but pursued by her fiancé's young illigitimate brother (played by Ivor). Sent out of England by the fiancé, Ivor met his love again in China, where she was appearing in an amateur version of one of her great successes! The plot grows yet more complex and unlikely; there is an earthquake, the hero and his love spend the night (asleep) together in an ancient temple, where they dream an eastern ballet, are then captured by rebels, but escape in time to be married on a Bridge of Lovers.

Audiences – indeed, critics – were less likely to resent plots of such complexity and unreality in 1936 than they are today; but it is none the less surprising that *The Times* complimented Ivor on 'imposing a unity rare in musical plays'! *The Sunday Times* admired his acting, as well as his wit and musicality; *Variety* called the show 'the best of its kind ever conceived'.

It remains probably the weakest of his eight musicals. The score contains 'Why is there Ever Goodbye?', which Olive Gilbert sang in her thrillingly forthright contralto; for Dorothy Dickson there was 'Music in May', but it was Ivor's presence and the production, again by Leontine Sagan, that drew the crowds – the Chinese Ballet (in which, for a while, Ivor actually danced) in a splendid temple set; a spectacular shop interior in Bond Street;

Ivor Novello and Dorothy Dickson in the Temple Ballet from *Careless Rapture* (1936). Novello's ability as a dancer was perhaps the least of his many talents, but his costume is sensational. Note the elasticated boots.

Hampstead Heath and its fair (a scene for which Ivor wrote three pastiches of Cockney knees-up songs which were highly effective); and of course the earthquake scene, with the devastation of a Chinese city.

And as for the finale – it was the epitome of Ivor finales: the set was almost entirely in white. An enormous bridge spanned the stage to a Chinese temple; near it stood the chorus, all in white, with Olive Gilbert and Dorothy Dickson . . . and into the scene staggered Ivor, having escaped from the rebels, travel-worn, tattered and weary, to find happiness in the arms of his virginal bride. The audience on the first night went wild with excitement and pleasure.

In tackling his third big show for Drury Lane, Ivor, despite his great self-confidence, must have felt something of a tremor. Yet another success might be too much to ask for. He once more wrote with specific performers in mind – many of them members of the Novello Operatic and Dramatic Society: Dorothy Dickson, Olive Gilbert, Peter Graves, Walter Chrisham, Maidie Andrews and Minnie Rayner (who was his 'mascot': she had appeared first with him in *Symphony in Two Flats* in 1929, and was to be in almost all the Novello entertainments until her death).

Crest of the Wave was produced during Coronation Year – 1937. Its plot was even more unlikely than that of *Careless Rapture*; an impoverished English duke, having been shot four times by a disappointed lady friend, survives to become a film-star, and to marry a beautiful young woman who is badly injured in a train crash (interjected as the now mandatory 'big effect' expected in most Drury Lane shows, and every Novello musical). The last scene reads so excruciatingly that it is difficult to believe it could ever have been played without provoking giggles: 'I cannot tell you how deeply I regret that Her Grace cannot be with you', says the Duke; 'perhaps next year . . . the doctors are afraid she may never walk again.' Whereupon, enter, downstage left, Miss Dickson – to enormous applause, and walking without the aid of crutches. The scene is rather typical of Novello's books: if ever musicals succeeded despite their dramatic element, his are prime examples.

Ivor's personality carried, in this case, not only the preposterous plot, but a musical almost entirely without effective numbers. Edgar Eames sang 'Rose of England', a song which survived to be popular for over thirty years, and Olive Gilbert had a success with 'The Haven of My Heart', in a scene which also contained a ballet choreographed by Lydia Sokolova and Anthony Tudor. But the score, apart from that, is undistinguished. Ivor, however, amply satisfied his fans, playing not only the hero but the villain – a disappointed Hollywood star who engineers the train crash, yet again filling the Drury Lane stage with smouldering wreckage.

'One staggers out', *The Observer* remarked rather unkindly, 'sated and a trifle stunned, observing, with a bloated species of relief, as one does at the end of a long Christmas dinner with the family, that this occasion is over for another year.' The applause on the first night was perhaps slightly less full-throated than on the two previous occasions; and indeed, *Crest of the Wave* only ran for six months before going out on tour – with an unknown, a young dancer called Roma Beaumont, replacing Dorothy Dickson. Miss Beaumont, Ivor announced, was 'the girl for whom he was writing his next play'.

That play was *The Dancing Years* – his most successful musical. Compare the list of numbers with the scores of any of his other musicals, and the contrast is marked: there is scarcely an unknown title among them – 'Waltz of My Heart', 'The Wings of Sleep', 'My Life Belongs to You', 'I Can Give You the Starlight', 'My Dearest Dear', 'Primrose', 'The Leap Year Waltz' . . .

Ivor always seemed a man utterly engrossed in the theatre, and as Sandy Wilson has pointed out in his *Ivor*, one of the surprising things about *The Dancing Years* is that it contained a protest against Germany's treatment of the Jews (though the management of Drury Lane objected that this was out of place in a musical, and attempted to persuade him to remove the relevant scene). The plot was as romantic as all Ivor's plots: a star of the Vienna Opera (played by Mary Ellis) discovered a young composer in a country inn, took him up, and became his mistress. Unknown to her, he had promised to give first refusal of his hand to the innkeeper's little niece, Grete (Roma Beaumont), when she grew up. She refused – but the prima donna, pregnant with his child, overheard, and in a rage married her former lover, Prince Charles Metterling.

After many years, the successful composer and the ageing prima donna met again, admitted that they were still in love, but parted when he realised that he could not ask her to abandon her marriage or to admit the illigitimacy of their son. In the last controversial scene set in 'the present', the composer was condemned to death by the Nazis for helping Jews to escape from Austria (the Lane management finally allowed this on condition that the Germans wore anonymous uniforms, and that there was no reference to Hitler). At the last minute, the composer was saved by Prince Metterling's intervention.

From the first, there was no doubt that the show was to be a success. The press was unanimous in praise of Ivor, Mary Ellis, Roma Beaumont (who stopped the show with 'Primrose', a pastiche of an Edwardian musical comedy number), and the rest of the cast – Olive Gilbert and Peter Graves, as usual, among them. *The Dancing Years* opened on March 23, 1939. On August 31, Novello went down to the footlights and invited a tiny audience to collect together in the stalls, rather than sit in lonely scattered twosomes through the theatre. It was the last night of that first production. Three days later, war was declared.

The Dancing Years was too good to vanish, even in those difficult times.

Drury Lane, during the war, became the headquarters of ENSA, the organisation which was set up to bring entertainment to the troops, and which they ungratefully entitled Every Night Something Awful. In 1940, a production of *The Dancing Years* was sent out on tour, and in 1942 came into town to the Adelphi Theatre, where it ran for over two years with Muriel Barron in the lead, and with most of the original cast.

The play displays Ivor's strength and weakness in fairly equal quantities: the romanticism now seems overblown if not slightly comic, and while the melodies themsleves are as beguiling as ever, the orchestration sounds thin and the lyrics banal. Christopher Hassall's line in romance was akin to Ivor's own: his rhymes were intensely romantic and traditional:

> I can give you the starlight,
> Love unchanging and true.
> I can give you the ocean,
> Deep and tender devotion.
> I can give you the mountains,
> Pools of shimmering blue.
> Call and I shall be
> All you ask of me –
> Music in Spring,
> Flowers for a King,
> All these I bring to you.

But there was simplicity that was affecting, especially when set to Ivor's swooning music:

> My dearest dear,
> If I could say to you
> In words as clear
> As when I play to you,
> You'd understand
> How slight the shadow that is holding us apart.
> So take my hand,
> I'll lead the way for you;
> A little waiting and you'll reach my heart.

And there can be no doubt that Hassall and Ivor saw eye to eye as far as attitudes were concerned. Take, for instance, 'Uniform', the number for the officers in *The Dancing Years*:

> We've got a uniform for riding in the ring.
> We've got a uniform for bowing to a King.
> We've got a uniform for every duty we fulfil –
> Ladies still from our drill get a thrill.
> And when they ask us what we think about the war,
> We all admit we can't imagine what it's for.
> So we dress up in all our finery each night and day –
> Then we play, shout and say, 'Let's be Gay!'

There can be little doubt that Ivor's view of men in uniform is adequately mirrored in that lyric: Cole Lesley remembers the occasion when Ivor and Noël Coward were sitting together in a news cinema watching the film of Mr Chamberlain's return after Munich, waving the celebrated piece of paper bearing Hitler's signature and his own. Infuriated beyond words by Britain's betrayal of her Allies, Coward turned to Ivor to comment, and saw tears of joy streaming down his face. At which, he hit him.

But that had been four years ago, and by 1943 Ivor was at work on another musical – for Mary Ellis, absent from the musical stage since the first run of *The Dancing Years*. As his theme, he took the life of the American operatic star Mary Garden. He made her a Frenchwoman, and gave her a young lover, an actor who becomes a film-star.He is alienated from her when she accepts the 'protection' of an impresario, and later killed on the Western Front during the First World War.

Arc de Triomphe opened in November, 1943. It had several limitations, one of which was that Ivor himself did not appear in it. There were a couple of good numbers – 'Paris Reminds Me of You', which Peter Graves sang and danced, and a quieter number, 'Dark Music', sung by Elizabeth Welch. But it is badly constructed (the hero is dead before the evening is half over), and the lack of spectacular effects was no help. The final blow to the show was the bad publicity when Ivor, in April 1944, was sentenced to eight weeks' imprisonment for a petty infringement of the Motor Vehicles Order restricting the use of petrol for private purposes during the war.

It was a minor 'crime', and Ivor seems to have been led into it by an over-zealous woman admirer and by his love of comfort and his own Rolls-Royce. It did him no permanent harm with his public; indeed, when he returned to the cast of *The Dancing Years* after his release, he received such a welcome that he remarked to Sir Edward Marsh that he felt he must have come back from Normandy with the VC rather than having done 'a spot of time'. But *Arc de Triomphe* had by then closed after only a short run, losing money – though that was no great financial blow to Ivor, whose earnings for 1942-3 totalled almost £37,000 before tax.

The next musical, *Perchance to Dream*, was composed mostly during an ENSA tour in Europe. Ivor composed many of his shows while touring with the previous ones. Indeed, occasionally he would startle the cast by playing, in one of the many scenes he wrote with himself at the piano, totally unfamiliar music which turned out to be from a score in preparation. *Perchance to Dream*, which opened at the Hippodrome in April 1945, had the longest run of any Novello show – 1020 performances. Once again, the performers were familiar: Ivor himself, Roma Beaumont, Muriel Barron, Olive Gilbert, Bobby Andrews – joined by Margaret Rutherford. The plot concerned a Regency buck, also a highwayman, who wagers £5000 that he will seduce an unknown cousin within a day of her coming to visit him. But

of course he falls in love with her, and when he dies at the end of Act I, the audience was only temporarily shattered; for he returned, reincarnated, to have continuing affairs with his love up through the ages until 'the present'.

Once more, Ivor wrote an incorrigibly romantic story – and this time the score was much more solid: 'We'll Gather Lilacs' remains one of his best known songs; 'Love is my Reason' is a fine waltz-song; Olive Gilbert sang 'Highwayman Love' with a vigour that won the audience; and 'A Woman's Heart' was a winning romantic number. 'The curtain, when it went up, took with it the entire audience', wrote James Agate in *The Sunday Times*, 'which remained in a seventh heaven until, after three hours and a half, the curtain descended and automatically brought the audience down with it.'

It was during the run of *Perchance to Dream* that Ivor heard an understudy singing in a touring production of *The Dancing Years*, and made a perhaps unconscious decision to write a piece for her. She was one Ruby Moule; Ivor renamed her Vanessa Lee. The musical comedy he wrote for her was *King's Rhapsody*. Once more, most of the score was written on tour – with *Perchance to Dream,* in South Africa. Vanessa Lee has recalled hearing 'Someday my Heart will Awake' on-stage during the first act of the former show, in a scene in which Ivor, playing the highwayman, was supposed to be improvising at the piano! He seems to have conceived the show as a final farewell to Ruritania – and perhaps his own last appearance in a musical of his own, for this time he appeared as an ageing man – Crown Prince Nikki of Murania, in exile for the sake of his mistress. Nikki agrees to undergo a diplomatic marriage with a Princess whom, in fact, he seduces, believing her to be a maid! Having borne him a son, but been studiously ignored, she finally captivates him when they are both involved in a peasant rising. There are the usual Ruritanian complications; but the show had a heart-wringing ending when Ivor, after the coronation of the boy-king, his son, walked incognito into the deserted cathedral to pick up the single white rose dropped there on the altar steps by his love.

By the time *King's Rhapsody* opened in London – at the Palace, in September 1949 – the face of musical comedy had changed completely. London was in the middle of its love affair with the American musical – *Oklahoma!* had taken the town by storm two years earlier; *Annie Get Your Gun* consolidated its success at the Coliseum. The older generation of English musical comedy composers were feeling the draught: Noël Coward, Ivor's friend, had had one failure with *Pacific 1860*, now had another with *Ace of Clubs*, and wrote to his friend Cole Lesley: 'I am furious about *Ace of Clubs* not being a real success, and I have come to the conclusion that if they

Muriel Barron looks on as Ivor Novello embraces Margaret Rutherford in *Perchance to Dream* (1945). This 'musical romance' was precisely the kind of escapism needed after six years of war.

don't care for first rate music, lyrics, dialogue and performance, they can stuff it up their collective arses and go and see *King's Rhapsody* until les vaches se rentrent . . .'

And indeed 'they' *did* come to *King's Rhapsody*, and without much persuasion, for it had Ivor's best score since *The Dancing Years*, including 'Someday My Heart Will Awake', 'Fly Home, Little Heart', 'If This Were Love', 'The Mayor of Perpignan' (left over from an earlier score), 'Take Your Girl', and 'The Violin Began to Play'. 'Sweet tooth is sweetly served, and, what is more, abundantly', wrote *The Observer*. 'The master touch was stronger than ever', said the *Daily Mirror*. 'Just the desired blend of champagne and sugar', suggested the *Daily Mail*. Opinions were not unanimous: if some critics had felt, in the twenties and thirties, that the Novello touch was over-romantic, it was not surprising that in 1949 Milton Schulman in the *Evening Standard* should have found that *King's Rhapsody* 'drips with cloying sentiment, that its situations are contrived and ludicrous, and that it is practically empty of wit'; or that *Punch* found the show 'a vast insipid musical in which Mr Ivor Novello has pulled out most of the known stops in the organ of easy sentiment'. But the general opinion was that of *The Sunday Times* – that if the piece 'might be supposed to embody the ultimate in saccherine banality . . . the result is an uncommonly pleasant evening in the theatre'.

Though obviously unwell, looking exhausted and older than his years, Ivor played in *King's Rhapsody* until the evening of March 5, 1951. Then he had a light supper with his friend Tom Arnold, the impresario; went back to the flat in the Aldwych; and died in the very early hours of the next morning, with Bobby Andrews and Olive Gilbert at his bedside.

Less than three weeks earlier, he had been at the Saville Theatre for the first night of *Gay's the Word*, which he wrote for Cecile Courtneidge – an enormously successful show for which Alan Melville wrote the lyrics. Once more, though the score was not one of his best, there were good numbers – 'Vitality', which Miss Courtneidge sang with such gusto, and 'Finder, Please Return', for Lizabeth Webb, one of his most graceful songs.

Ivor Novello was the last of the true line of musical comedy composers to work in England. Though in *Gay's the Word* he made a brave, deliberate attempt – on the whole, successful – to write a show more of the fifties (slick and breezy), it may be that he would have found it difficult to maintain his success in the sixties; in any event, he was fifty-eight when he died, and may have been losing some of his inventiveness and facility, though there was little sign of this in *King's Rhapsody*. The work he did was in a medium which is no less of the past than the shows of the Gaiety and Daly's in the early years of the century – and anyone under forty will perhaps find it difficult, despite the melodic strength of his best songs, to understand how he could have been so popular. There is so little evidence left.

Two films were made of his musicals. *Glamorous Night*, made in 1937 with Mary Ellis and Barry McKay, was a disaster. The plot was altered (the hero became an oil prospector – perhaps because films could not bring themselves to recognise the very existence of their rival, television!). There was talk of dictatorships and concentration camps, and the direction and settings were slow and unkempt. The film of *The Dancing Years*, in which Dennis Price played the Novello part, was a little better. Patricia Dainton played Roma Beaumont's part, and Vanessa Lee dubbed the singing voice of the prima donna, played by Gisèle Préville. Neither of these films conveys anything of the charm and attraction of the originals: and of course, Ivor himself was absent from them, for some unexplained reason.

A reading of the books and lyrics adds nothing. It cannot be denied that Ivor's stage-plays themselves are no longer really acceptable to modern audiences, and the books of his musicals are even worse – carelessly written, poorly constructed, charmless and witless. The lyrics – most of them by Christopher Hassall, though Ivor wrote the lyrics as well as the book of *King's Rhapsody* – are passable but little more. The intangible element which reconciled audiences to the plays was Ivor himself; and a combination of his personality and music made his musicals live.

As to that music itself: it is a strange phenomenon. When he wrote a short extract from an opera, supposedly about Joan of Arc, which was sung at one of the climaxes of *Arc de Triomphe*, Ivor was expressing a long-felt ambition. After he had accompanied Olive Gilbert to a performance of one of Gian-Carlo Menotti's operas, he confided to her that it was his ambition to write a full-scale opera. Without doubt, it would have been a disaster. His gift for simple melody is unquestionable, and cannot seriously be in doubt. His musical education and grasp of technique was as near nil as makes no difference. The full-scale semi-operatic Coronation Scene at the end of *King's Rhapsody* is a weak imitation of Gounod at his worst, seventy or eighty years out of date even as a pastiche.

He composed at the piano. If a tune did not come spontaneously when uninvited, he went and did something else, and let the tune come when it would. He much admired Puccini, Debussy, and Wagner, and traces of their influence appear in his best work. But all his music went to a professional orchestrator (so, of course, did Noël Coward's); and it was not always very well scored at that – woodwind, for instance, hardly every played a part in the arrangements.

Ivor knew that people looked forward to 'a lovely tune', and that is what he concentrated on – to the extent of lazily neglecting the introductions and verses of his numbers. But when the big tunes came, everything was forgiven. He wrote well for the voice, especially the voice he knew, curving the tunes instinctively to suit them. The best of his songs – 'Love is My

Reason for Living' is an example – are melodically as good as anything written by his contemporaries.

Finally, there was himself as an actor. He was a fine technician, whether in melodrama, romance or comedy. Unprofessional in some ways – he was very prone to giggling on stage, to playing up to friends who happened to be 'in front', to ignoring his director – he could pull off a good scene when he had one, and saw to it that in plays of his own, he had plenty. He was, it seems, an almost incorrigibly *nice* man. I have never met anyone who has a serious word of criticism for him as a friend or actor (apart from a tendency to be close with his money). This niceness came across the footlights, and allied to his charm and appearance – a matter almost entirely of profile, for he was not particularly well-formed – positively attracted more hero-worship from fans than any other male star of his period. He also carefully cultivated a certain nobility of manner, off-stage as well as on; allegedly, the late Queen Mary commented that he was the only actor she had ever seen, who was able to give an adequate indication of 'what it meant to be Royal'.

If one is to judge him by other masters of operetta or musical comedy, it must be said that in the final analysis he does not come in the top ten; he has not the musical inventiveness, let alone the technique, of Léhar or Kálmán, and his books and lyrics lack the real wit and ingenuity of Cole Porter or of Coward at his best. He contributed many enjoyable pages to the history of 'the musical', without in the very least contributing to its development, and without at all influencing any other writer or composer. It could be argued, I suppose, that by presenting outworn ideas in an outworn *genre*, he contributed firmly to the death of that *genre*.

But still and all, the enjoyment he gave to millions of people (many of whom had never seen him in the flesh) is excuse enough to earn him the niche which he firmly holds in British light music; his bust stands still in Drury Lane Theatre – and no-one has a better right to its place.

7

A. P. H. and Vivian Ellis

'At nineteen I became a retired businessman . . .' — VIVIAN ELLIS

When Tantivy Towers was produced at the Lyric Theatre, Hammersmith, in January, 1931, it was for a moment thought that a new Gilbert and Sullivan partnership had been born – for it brought together a 'serious' composer, Thomas F. Dunhill, and one of the liveliest, wittiest of English essayists and versifiers, A. P. Herbert. Somehow the alchemy failed to work, but Herbert went on to write, with Vivian Ellis, some of the most charming musical plays of the next twenty years.

Herbert was born in September 1890. His mother had come from a Church family – 'a long line of Anglican Bishops', A. P. H. used to say – and his father from a Catholic Irish family. He was educated at Winchester and Oxford, and began writing verse at the age of sixteen – a passion which was never to desert him. He even made public speeches in verse, and replied in iambic couplets when he was given an honorary degree at Oxford in 1958. But he also wrote in prose: his first book was *The Secret Battle*, which came out of his experiences in the Navy during the First World War. It was not a commercial success, but was critically well received, and is indeed a small classic of its kind. His comic characters Topsy (inventor of the phrase 'It's the done thing') and the litigious Mr Haddock are part of the great canon of English humour.

A. P. H. (who signed his many contributions to *Punch* with his initials) based his reputation as a librettist on his accomplishments as a writer of light verse. He wrote a very great deal of it – for a quarter of a century he contributed a topical poem every week to the *Sunday Graphic* – and practice certainly made almost perfect. He loved music, and naturally conceived an enormous admiration for the Savoy Operas, though he was later to believe that he was a rather better librettist than W. S. Gilbert, being more adept and classical in his rhyming, and a good deal kinder to his characters. Like Gilbert, he was a purist, and took great care over his rhymes. The whole idea of assonance, introduced into modern English poetry by Wilfred Owen, was a blank to him, and he was often heard to castigate the moderns for their false quantities and false rhymes, berating Noël Coward for instance for rhyming 'Malta' with 'falter' and 'circus' with 'mazurkas'.

His neat rhymes soon began to appear in *Punch* and elsewhere, and some of them became very well-known indeed: he had the distinction of being rebuked by the House of Commons for circulating, during the Second World War, a verse opposing a second front; he greeted Winston Churchill in verse when the two men passed each other in mid-Atlantic during the war; and, in the end, he confessed to being the author of the most popular and best-known set of obscene verses written in our own time, the notorious 'Portions of a Woman' (originally entitled 'Lines on a Book Borrowed from the Ship's Doctor'):

> The portions of a woman which appeal to man's depravity
>   Are constructed with considerable care,
> And what appears to you to be a simple little cavity
>   Is really an elaborate affair . . .

A. P. H.s wife's cousin was the composer Roger Quilter, and there was at one time talk of their writing a musical play together; but it came to nothing. However, with hindsight, it seems inevitable that the musical theatre should have captured him – and indeed, he was to write the words for fifteen full-length musical revues and plays, and four short ones, between 1924 and his death in 1975.

His first effort, in 1924, was a Christmas play entitled *King of the Castle*, for the Playhouse, Liverpool; the music was by Dennis Arundell, and the piece was commissioned by William Armstrong, a well-known Edwardian actor and producer, later (like A. P. H. himself) knighted. It was very Gilbertian: children took over the office of Blunderbuss and Cheese, stockbrokers, in the first act, and turned their attention to running the grown-ups' affairs. The provincial critics greeted it with enthusiasm, talking of its perhaps taking the place of *Peter Pan* as a Christmas entertainment. That was never to happen – indeed, the play never reached London – but the libretto does show A. P. H.'s deft touch, as in a song for Mr Cheese, in which he regrets the necessity for travel by sea:

> But Ah, how short a step is there
> From high romance to *mal de mer*!
> The nation, Sir, that lifts a hand
> Against our well-beloved land,
> That race must reckon first with me,
> But anyone can have the sea!

A. P. H. was to write for revue (his best-known effort in that line was *Riverside Nights*, which reflected his great affection for the Thames, on whose bank he lived for the best part of half-a-century); he was to turn out the English libretti for Offenbach operettas – *La Vie Parisienne* and *La Belle Helene* (produced by C. B. Cochran as *Helen!*, with George Robey as Menelaus); and he was to write light plays in verse, the best of which is

Shocked members of a Hunt look on as their Master holds aloft the corpse of a fox shot by the hero (Trefor Jones) of A. P. Herbert's *Tantivy Towers* (1931). Equally shocked by the author's attack on the world of huntin', shootin' and fishin', some members of the audience left the theatre before the end of the operetta.

perhaps *Two Gentlemen of Soho*, an excellent parody of Shakespeare produced in tandem with Sheridan's *The Critic*, in 1927.

But it was with *Tantivy Towers* that he found his feet as an original writer of both book and lyrics. Like everything else he wrote for the stage, it had its own satirical point: the conflict between the Counties and Chelsea, between blood-sports and Bohemia. Lady Ann Gallop (Barbara Pett Frazer) falls in love with handsome, golden-voiced tenor Hugh Heather (Trefor Jones), hired to entertain the guests at Tantivy Hall on the occasion of a hunting weekend. Her friends and admirers do not take to this interloping artist: Lord Bareback is unequivocal –

> Lord Tantivy, I must insist
> On horsewhipping this vocalist!

But he is persuaded to keep quiet while Hugh sings – tactfully choosing 'John Peel', which thrills the assembled Hunt. But when he is invited to join the chase on the following morning, Hugh declines, and in an admirable set-piece sings of his reasons, while the huntsmen, growing more and more restive, interrupt his song with snatches of 'John Peel'. Hugh's long solo is one of the most remarkable numbers ever inserted into an operetta (for that is what *Tantivy Towers* is; there is no spoken dialogue at all). It pulls no punches:

> Listen! I will go riding where you will!
> I love the horse – though I have not your skill.
> But do not ask me to enjoy
> This pretty sport, for, as a boy,

I've seen your butchers' work, and had my fill.
You fouled the charming country's breath
With scent of blood and boast of death,
While every spinney blushed for shame
To be a partner in the game!

In the end, Hugh and Ann part, and the Hunt wins. But it is not a victory without wounds, and it is not surprising that many of A. P. H.'s friends in society failed to enjoy the piece, leaving shortly after Hugh's solo.

Thomas Dunhill, who set *Tantivy Towers* to music, had studied composition under C. V. Stanford, and had been an assistant music master at Eton. He had a very considerable reputation as a chamber music composer, and a writer of songs – his setting of W. B. Yeats' 'The Cloths of Heaven' is a minor masterpiece of its period. Just as A. P. H. admired Gilbert and Sullivan, so did Dunhill; indeed, he wrote an excellent book about the Savoy operas – so it is not surprising that there was much talk of 'the new G. and S.' In a sense, however, Dunhill was too ambitious a musician to be a success in collaboration with A. P. H. He was more at home in his other light opera, *Happy Families*, for which the libretto was written by Rose Fyleman; but that was only produced out of town, at Guildford, in 1933 – the book was not as accomplished as the music.

There were no tunes in the score of *Tantivy Towers* ingratiating enough to take the town; and Dunhill's musical sensitivity was such that he let some opportunities pass him by. For a scene in a Chelsea artist's studio, for instance, he neglected to write anything approaching the jazz for which a party scene called. On the other hand, his 'Where the Merry Artists Gather' has some of the charm of Sullivan, and in the hunt-supper scene Dennis Arundell as the M. F. H. stopped the show with a robust ballad, 'Ride Straight'. Musically, there is an absolutely splendid set-piece when a trio of footmen rebuke Hugh, who has shot a hunted fox. Again, A. P. H. honed the edge of his wit:

There are some things which are not done:
To shoot a fox of course is one.
But the offence is fouler still
If hounds are just about to kill:
For this is nothing, we conclude,
But robbing hungry dogs of food:
And persons who torment a pet
Deserve whatever they may get.

Dunhill wrote a lugubrious setting for the verses, sung by the three footmen standing in a small grim group near the footlights; extremely memorable.

A. P. H.'s second musical, *Derby Day*, followed *Tantivy Towers* thirteen months later, in February of 1932, and was produced at the Lyric for

£1000 – a small sum even for those days. The music was by the resident conductor of the orchestra at that theatre, Alfred Reynolds, and its heroes, A. P. H. said in a Prologue which he himself recited from the stage on the first night, were the ordinary people:

We have defied the canons of the age
And put the British people on the stage.
Prepare your shoulders with the rough to rub:
Most of the action centres in a pub.
Our heroine is not as others are,
But works those engines just behind the bar:
And you may nominate for leading man
Either a tipster or a publican.

Derby Day was nothing if not colourful: there was a pub-full of costers in their 'pearlies', a scene at Epsom racecourse, and one in the stables where, outside the favourite's stall, a number of villains gathered together aiming to influence the horse by singing at it! A. P. H. had, as usual, his special targets: there is a baronet who keeps horses but disapproves of betting, his son, an undergraduate who messes about with a barmaid, and his interfering lady, 'a magistrate, a councillor, a mother and a wife', in that order. The Licencing Board was dragged into the last act in order that the author should make his protest against the stupidity of the English licencing laws (against which he made many sorties during his career as a Member of Parliament).

There were one or two good numbers: Tessa Deane sang 'I Wish I Didn't Like You' to great effect, and there was some good music for the drinkers and punters, and for Bert the tipster:

Every time your 'orses start
'Arf the country breaks its 'eart:
The other 'arf they comes in 'ere
And stands the other 'arf a beer.

And there was a solo in which the Baronet apostrophised his putative winner with the magnificent opening couplet:

Beloved horse, attend, I pray;
The Derby will be run today!

Then Mrs Bones, played by a favourite character actress, Mabel Constanduros, who became famous on radio during the war, started off with a song extolling the virtues of orange juice, and ended by walking out with the publican.

But the sad truth of the matter was that once again the composer with whom A. P. H. had worked was simply not a natural for the *genre*. Alfred Reynolds had studied in Berlin and Paris under Humperdinck, and as a young man had conducted a great deal of opera in Paris and London.

Though he became a conductor for George Edwardes and later for Sir Barry Jackson and Sir Nigel Playfair, and had worked with A. P. H. on *Riverside Nights*, one feels that his heart was in more 'serious' work. His real success, and his only one in light music, was to be with the incidental music for *1066 and All That*. *Derby Day*, as James Agate was to point out in *The Sunday Times*, simply didn't seem to capture his musical imagination in the right way. When it was chucking-out time in the pub, Mr Agate pointed out, 'Mr Reynolds replies with a phrase worthy of *The Immortal Hour*', and 'after three hours of striving has not produced a single tune which the commonalty will recognise as such'.

After the great success of *Helen!* for C. B. Cochran came *Mother of Pearl*, a straight play with a few of Oscar Straus' songs inserted into it, for which A. P. H. wrote the lyrics. That was in 1933. The following year, Herbert first met with Vivian Ellis, with whom he was to write his best musicals. Cochran engaged them both to contribute to *Streamline*, a revue featuring Florence Desmond.

Ellis was born in 1904, and his mother was an intensely musical woman; so had her family been, at least from her grandfather's time, who made and lost two fortunes in the West Indies, selling musical instruments to the natives! His maternal grandmother, Julia Woolf, was a composer whose *Carina* was produced, at the Opera Comique, The Strand, in 1888; a friend of Sir Arthur Sullivan's, she was also a pianist who performed at Promenade Concerts at Covent Garden Opera House in the eighties and nineties.

Ellis' mother studied the violin at the Brussels Conservatoire under Ysaye, and was said to have played the violin every day while she was pregnant, hoping for a musical child. Her wish was granted. Young Vivian performed his first scale at the age of five, earning a penny from his father. He was substantially brought up by his mother, after his father's early death; during his time at school he wrote at the age of eight a piece of programme music describing the sinking of the Titanic; and he had a distinct talent for the piano, which made itself apparent to the teacher, Stanley Ormandy, when, at a pupils' concert, young Ellis started by accident to play Rachmaninov's Prelude in C sharp minor in the key of C minor by mistake, and continued triumphantly to finish the whole piece a semi-tone down.

Ormandy immediately took him as a pupil. When he left school there was considerable pressure on him to enter his father's tailoring business (of which, by the terms of his Will, he was to become a senior partner at the age of twenty-one). But music was his interest. He continued playing the piano with great determination, studied under Myra Hess, took harmony and counterpoint with Emma Lomax, and had played concertos with a local orchestra – the West Pier Orchestra at Brighton, where the family lived – before the time came when he was forced to don a bowler hat and go daily to the office in London.

His incarceration there did not last long. He firmly negotiated his release from the business and at the age of nineteen I became a retired businessman' with his eye firmly fixed on the musical stage. He fervently admired Paul Rubens, André Messager, Reynaldo Hahn and Jerome Kern, and through a number of tough years continued to write music in his own idiom, declining to write what other people thought he should write – which included everything from the ballads which Ivor Novello was then popularising to the new syncopated music from the U.S. Soon, he was edging songs into revues, and was invited in 1925 to write some material for Jack Hulbert's new show *By the Way,* which ran for 341 performances at the Apollo.

By 1927, he had had songs in several West End revues. Cochran gave him some work; he wrote the music for *Palladium Pleasures*, and for a touring musical play, *The Call of the Legion*, adapted from a P. C. Wren novel. In 1928, he began working on a musical play called *The Flower Princess* (as the result of being placed under contract by Chappell & Co., the music publishers). That project fell through, but then came the offer of a script entitled *Mr Cinders*, a play by Clifford Grey and Greatrex Newman which had originally been written for Leslie Henson and Violet Loraine. Now, with Binnie Hale in mind, Ellis composed a delightful score for it, which contained his first great hit, 'Spread a Little Happiness'.

Mr Cinders also starred Bobby Howes, and was in some ways his most successful musical. The story was that of Cinderella with the sexes reversed: Cinderella was Jim Lancaster, a rather downtrodden cousin of some snobbish aristocrats. Jill Kemp (Binnie Hale) arrived on the scene – a millionaire's daughter on the run from the police, pursuing her for a driving offence – and sent Lancaster off to the ball in fancy-dress, accompanying him in her Rolls. The pair worked together perfectly, Howes encouraging Binnie Hale to off-set with her dazzling good looks the rather overpowering effect of the larger women in the cast who had been bullying him. When they sang 'I'm a One-Man Girl who's Looking for a One-Girl Man', they stopped the show.

Mr Cinders opened at the Adelphi in February 1929, made a profit of £800 in its first week, and settled into a successful run. Ellis was called in to replace Ivor Novello (whose composing muse had temporarily deserted him) to write the music for Beverley Nichols' words in Cochran's 1930 Pavilion revue. 'The Wind in the Willows' was one of the numbers, which the black entertainer Hutch recorded with great success.

Ellis was by now very much in demand: so much so that in 1930 he found himself involved in one way or another with no fewer than six new West End musical shows. *Follow a Star*, for Sophie Tucker, was about a cabaret, and besides Miss Tucker had Jack and Claude Hulbert, Alfred Drayton and Betty Ann Davis in the cast. For Miss Tucker, Ellis wrote the tearjerking

One of the most popular duos of musical comedy in the '20s and '30s – Binnie Hale is comforted by Bobby Howes in Vivian Ellis' *Mr Cinders* (1929).

'When Your Kisses Can't Hold the Man You Love then Your Tears Won't Bring Him Back'! Having got that out of the way, Ellis turned to *Little Tommy Tucker,* for Daly's, with a book and lyrics by four different writers. Completing the music for it, he started on *Stand Up and Sing,* contributing five songs to the ten supplied by Phil Charig. Jack Buchanan and Elsie Randolph, Roma Beaumont, Richard Murdoch and Anna Neagle were in the cast, and the show ran for some considerable time. Then Ellis completed

Binnie Hale in *Mr Cinders* here resembles more a chorus-girl escaped from one of Busby Berkeley's elaborate musical films.

the music for *Folly to be Wise,* a revue for Cecily Courtneidge.

Follow a Star opened at the Winter Garden in September 1930, and had a good press; but ran for only 118 performances. *Little Tommy Tucker* at Daly's ran for only eighty-six performances after its opening, in November of the same year. *Folly to be Wise,* however, was a real success, opening at the Piccadilly in January 1931, and running for 257 performances: James Agate wrote that the score was 'the most knavishly witty music imaginable'.

The Song of the Drum opened at Drury Lane in January, 1931. The story, by Guy Bolton and Fred Thompson, was about a revolt in one of Britain's colonies; there were regimental balls and gymkhanas, native bazaars and palaces, there were energetic dances choreographed by Ralph Reader, and there was a cast headed by Bobby Howes, Clarice Hardwicke and Derek Oldham. The leading lady, Helen Gilliland, was spectacularly miscast. As Ellis recalls in his memoirs, *I'm on a See-Saw*, 'to hear her say the lines "I was the woman in Captain Darrell's bedroom!" was to know that on the stage, at least, there was no possibility of her being in anybody's bedroom other than her own.'

There was some splendid scenery, one or two spectacular set-pieces, and one hit song, 'Within My Heart', sung by Marie Burke as a handsome Countess. The press was moderately kind, but the piece did not take on, and ran for only 131 performances.

The sixth show, *Blue Roses*, opened and closed at the Gaiety. It was booed by the gallery on its first night, and lasted for only fifty-four performances. One critic writing of Cochran's new revue actually said: 'One novelty I discovered is that Vivian Ellis will not compose the music.' His reputation slumped, and only Nigel Playfair invited him to work – to contribute the incidental music for a stage adaptation of Evelyn Waugh's novel *Vile Bodies* for the Arts Theatre.

Ellis claims that it was not long after this, in 1931, that he first – briefly – met A. P. Herbert, when he was asked to write a number called 'Little Boat' for Dora Labette to sing off-stage in Basil Dean's screen version of A. P. H.'s novel *The Water Gipsies*. The song went, almost twenty years later, into their last musical, a full stage version of the same novel.

But their true collaboration was still some time ahead. In the meantime, during the rest of the thirties, Ellis remained busy. In 1932, there was *Out of the Bottle*, based on F. Anstey's *The Brass Bottle*. Ellis worked on this with the American composer, part-time screen actor, and wise-cracker Oscar Levant. Produced at the London Hippodrome, it lasted for only one hundred performances. The same year – indeed, the same month – saw the first screening of a musical film for which Ellis wrote the score: *Jack's the Boy* starred Jack Hulbert and Cecily Courtneidge. Douglas Furber suggested the title of a song to Ellis, and the latter, realising the quality of film sound was such that nothing very sophisticated would stand a chance of being properly heard, 'sought a tune that would please a backward child of twelve', and in a few minutes jotted down a sixteen-bar chorus 'containing a choice of two chords, two arpeggios, and a five-finger exercise. "That" [he jeered] "is exactly what they want." ' The song was 'The Flies Crawled Up the Window', which sold a quarter of a million records, and was heard everywhere. The film itself was an enormous success, too.

In 1933, having contributed some songs to Charlot's revue *Please*, Ellis also published a novel, and wrote the score for *Jill Darling*, which opened the following year. It opened in Glasgow, as *Jack and Jill*, and did not please all the local critics, one of whom commented that 'there is little real musical virtue in Vivian Ellis' score, but he has the knack of pleasing the lazy and inefficient minds, if any, of the average musical comedy-goer. He gives them tunes sufficiently reminiscent to be instantly digested, and by his own craft converts them into almost equally instantaneous hits.' The reception was on the whole kindly, however, and when after a long tour and a change of cast it opened in London with a new title, and starring Frances Day and Arthur Riscoe, in December 1934, it was a hit. 'I'm on a See-Saw', sung by John Mills and Louise Browne, was the most popular number – it was recorded years later by Fats Waller! – and the show ran happily until Frances Day had to leave the cast to fulfil a film contract.

During the interval between the Glasgow production of *Jack and Jill* and the London production of *Jill Darling*, Ellis and A. P. H. had really got together, for the Cochran revue *Streamline*, to which Ronald Jeans also contributed. The first verses of A. P. H.'s which Ellis set (apart from 'The Little Boat') seem to have been his wistful 'Other People's Babies', which in fact was a poem rather than a lyric; it has been memorably performed nearer our own time by Joyce Grenfell.

The collaboration was successful right from the start. *Perseverance*, their parody of the Savoy operas, was wildly applauded by the critics who noticed *Streamline*, though it was too clever for the audiences. A burlesque of Amy Johnson went down better, performed by the brilliant Florence Desmond. The revue was a success.

More revues followed: *The Town Talks*, *Going Places*, *Hide and Seek* – and more hits, including the beautiful 'She's My Lovely'. In 1938, Ellis completed the score of *Running Riot*, for Leslie Henson, which played at the Gaiety, and was in fact the last show to be produced at that theatre. *Under Your Hat* was his last show before the war, during which, like A. P. H., Ellis served in the Navy, and had little to do with the theatre apart from producing a revue, *It's All Yours*, in the tiny and elegant Globe Theatre in the middle of the Marine Barracks at Devonport.

It was in September 1945 that Vivian Ellis' sister pointed out to him a small paragraph in a Sunday newspaper announcing that C. B. Cochran had received from Sir Alan Herbert the book of a new light opera. Rather tentatively, Ellis wrote to both Cochran and Herbert. Cochran had in fact approached William Walton to write the music; Walton had recommended Spike Hughes; but Hughes was not interested, and the script eventually reached Ellis. He had never written a light opera before, and indeed had written no music for six years; still, he read the script with interest. The show was called *Big Ben*.

A. P. H. had been the Independent Member of Parliament for Oxford

University since 1935. A gadfly always tickling the House's sense of humour, but also intensely serious and successful in ironing out some of the more insensitive and simply dotty quirks in the Law, he had come to venerate and love the place, and at last found it impossible to resist satirising it lovingly in a musical – as a sort of farewell, too, for the Independent University seats were soon to be abolished.

Basically, his book was about a romance between a Tory hero and a Socialist heroine, united in their opposition to a Bill aimed at prohibiting the sale of alcohol in England – a Bill which A. P. H. would have fought to the last breath, for as one of his lyrics announces:

> There's alcohol in plant and tree:
> It must be Nature's plan
> That there should be, in fair degree,
> Some alcohol in Man.

Boldly, A. P. H. took the action of the play right inside the Palace of Westminster. When Princess Elizabeth, attending her very first first night, Mr Winston Churchill, Lord Montgomery, and a crowd of Parliamentarians which made the stalls look like a magnified Treasury Bench, attended the opening night at the Adelphi on July 17, 1946, they saw a scene on the Terrace of the Commons, and another in the Chamber. Though the speaker was not seen, his voice was heard, and at the end of one scene the play's villains invaded the Chamber, kidnapped a Member and forcibly resisted the Serjeant-at-Arms.

A. P. H. was rather worried about the reactions of the Lord Chamberlain. When he asked Cochran what objections had been received, the latter went white, and said 'My God! – I never sent it to him!' However, when the script did return belatedly from the Chamberlain's office, there was only one objection – to a line spoken by a drinking M.P. to a teetotal woman M.P. who had complained of what drink did to the human stomach: 'I heard what the noble lady had to say about our stomachs. I tell the noble lady that I'll lay my stomach against her's any day.' The line was altered, though A. P. H. claimed to have heard it actually spoken in the House – to Lady Astor.

There is plenty of variety in the libretto of *Big Ben*, and plenty of action: the first act is set during a General Election, and ends with an election meeting. The heroine becomes a Labour Minister, but marries her Tory boy-friend and is locked up in the Tower with him. Ellis had a number of lively lyrics to set, including a stirring patriotic title-song (this was just after the end of the war):

> Big Ben! Big Ben! . . .
> The clock they could not kill,
> Chime out again and tell all men
> That England's England still . . .

A. P. Herbert and Vivian Ellis collaborated on four musical plays, of which *Bless the Bride* was the most successful. Here, in 1946, the composer looks over the author's shoulder as they consider the score of their first musical, *Big Ben*.

And there is a good number in defence of the House of Lords – for by this time the postwar Labour Government was of course discussing its abolition:

> While the Commons must bray like an ass every day
> To appease their electoral hordes,
> We don't say a thing till we've something to say –
> There's a lot to be said for the Lords.

At his home in Somerset, Vivian Ellis completed the score, and he and the author enjoyed rehearsals with the producer, Wendy Toye, Carole Lynne and Gabrielle Brune, with Joan Young, took the leading female roles, with Trefor Jones, David Davies, Eric Forte and Eric Palmer as the four leading men. Interestingly, Miss Lynne's understudy, who took over her part for some of the run, was a girl called Lizbeth Webb, who was later to be the star of *Bless the Bride*.

Big Ben opened to an enormously enthusiastic first-night audience for whom all the 'in' Parliamentary jokes were a treat. The Press, next morning, was less enthusiastic, comparing the work unfavourably to *Iolanthe*, Gilbert and Sullivan's Parliamentary operetta. The success of 'I Want to See the People Happy', the heroine's election manifesto, was undoubted, and David Davies sang splendidly Ellis' good number for the King's Bargemaster, 'London Town is Built on London's River' – another of A. P. H.'s tributes to the city and the Thames. But, the critics complained, the piece was more like a not very good Cochran revue than an operetta; the satire had no real cutting edge, and there was little force in the lyrics. It played nevertheless to over £4000 a week for three months; but two of the leading ladies left the cast early, and the play was withdrawn after only 172 performances.

It was while he was on holiday in Cornwall, staying on the Helford river, that A. P. H. wrote the first draft of his next musical, *Bless the Bride*. He sent a copy to Cochran and another to Ellis, in August 1946. Cochran had wanted a Victorian period piece, and in a bound volume of *Punch* for 1869 A. P. H. had seen drawings of bustled beauties playing croquet, and of the Franco-Prussian war in a later issue. So it was in that period that he set his new piece, with a Victorian family meeting in the first act to celebrate Grandpa's Golden Wedding and the wedding of his daughter Lucy. It is an intensely chauvinistic family, believing that the world only put up with foreigners 'till Heaven conceived a nobler plan, and made an Englishman'. But Lucy does not want to marry the stolid Englishman, Thomas Trout, to whom her family has promised her. Instead, she falls in love with Pierre, a handsome and spirited Frenchman, who carries her off to France while the family waits in church with her disappointed bridegroom. Grandpa promptly dies of grief and shame.

In Act II, the family follows Lucy to France, and finds her living in

Brian Reece, who gave a delightful performance as the Honourable Thomas Trout, is surrounded by a bevy of bridesmaids in *Bless the Bride* (1951), the best of the A. P. Herbert – Vivian Ellis musicals. It had a sparkling score and a witty and skillfully pointed plot.

delightful sin with her lover. But then the war breaks out, and Pierre puts on his uniform and leaves to defend Paris. She returns reluctantly to England, where she learns that Pierre has been killed during the Prussian attack. Once more, Thomas Trout and she approach the altar – but of course the handsome Pierre turns up at the last moment, and Trout, the rather pathetic, not ignoble young man who has longed to hear the world cry 'Well done, Trout!', gracefully retires and hands Lucy back to her lover.

Ellis and Herbert worked marvellously well together on the book and lyrics: not, however, without some twists and turns. The song 'I Was Never Kissed Before', one of the hits of the show, was set to words originally meant for a verse rather than a refrain. A. P. H. wrote three sets of lyrics for a song to be placed at one point in the play: concerning, in turn, a donkey, a soldier, and a girl. Eventually, it became that other hit 'Ma Belle Marguerite', sung by the handsome George Guétary, who became the darling of London:

> In September when the grapes are purple
> Marguerite pick the grapes with me.
> There are silver bells upon her fingers,
> All the little birds come out to see
> Ma belle Marguerite, so beautiful to see,
> Les mains de ma petite,
> Marguerite picking grapes with me . . .
>
> In December when the wind is blowing,
> When the snow is on the Bois d'Issy,
> Sunshine still is in the golden glasses –
> Marguerite drink the sun with me.

Then there was 'This Is My Lovely Day' (originally 'I Shall Remember This'), and 'O, What Will Mother Say?'

The show seemed from the start one of those happy ventures which cannot go wrong. In Paris, Ellis and Cochran found Guétary, a Greek (not, as everyone assumed, a Frenchman) who learned English especially for the production. Lizbeth Webb was immediately cast as Lucy, and Brian Reece, whom Ellis had heard performing during the war, was invited to play Trout – his first major West End part. Wendy Toye was to produce. Rehearsals went well, though there was a little trouble because Herbert (like Gilbert) liked his words to be heard, and (as Gilbert had found before him) singers are not always as audible verbally as musically.

Bless the Bride opened on a Saturday – June 11, 1949. Ellis, and for that matter Cochran, had had enough of musicals being injured by bad notices appearing on the morning after the first night. At least in this case word of mouth would have time to get around town before the notices appeared in the dailies on Monday. The critics were not over-kind: James Agate began his piece with the words *Ex nihilo magnum fit*, and *The Times* complained that though the show was fresh, it was far from original; on the other hand, it looked lovely, with 'all the charm of an ornate valentine painted and lavendered by artists whose taste demands respect.' Other critics complained that 'A. P. H. has given it just about as much plot as would go on the back of a cupronickel sixpence', 'he hardly troubles to find his play a plot', 'musically sugary and undistinguished', 'there is a lack of robust humour'.

Reading notices of musical comedy and operetta, one does tend to find that critics are unusually severe on the *genre* – perhaps because they do not seem to know quite how to take it. If a newspaper sends its music critic, he is all too obviously yearning for music at its heights, for scores of the calibre of *Die Fledermaus* at the best and the best of Offenbach at the least. If the drama critic goes, he is aghast at the simplicity of the plot and the vestigial nature of the characterisation. Very few modern operettas or musical comedies have escaped critical strictures on one side or the other – *A Little Night Music* is perhaps one example of a musical kindly received by both drama and music critics.

Ten days after the opening of *Bless the Bride*, another show opened at Drury Lane: *Oklahoma!* Six weeks later, it was joined, at the Coliseum, by *Annie Get Your Gun*. The three shows all ran happily and concurrently. *Bless the Bride* had over 800 performances, and, as Harold Hobson wrote: 'Sir Alan Herbert and Mr Vivian Ellis in "Ma Belle Marguerite" and "This Is My Lovely Day" in *Bless the Bride*, prove that Englishmen can still write songs as well as any people in the world; and *Oklahoma!* proves that Americans can do it as well as Englishmen.'

Tough at the Top, which opened in July 1949, was a relative failure. For this play, A. P. H. had decided on a plot about an affair between a Pomeranian princess and an English boxer at the turn of the century. Bored with the life of the Court, the Princess changes clothes with a Maid of Honour, and visits both the Derby and a prize-fight – where she falls instantly in love with one of the fighters, climbing into the ring to encourage him when he shows signs of flagging ('Kiss me, kiss me if you can, And I will kill this silly man', he promptly sings.) He is taken off to Pomerania to become Minister of Sport (a much-derided invention of A. P. H.'s which has subsequently become a commonplace), is involved in complex court intrigue, and decides that to triumph in the ring is not necessarily to triumph in life.

Vivian Ellis wrote some ambitious, perhaps over-ambitious, music for the piece; and Cochran decided that it must have absolutely first-rate singers at least in the major roles. In Paris, he and Ellis heard Maria d'Attili in a Menotti opera, and she agreed to play the Princess. Georgio Tozzi, who had lately been singing in an American production of Britten's *The Rape of Lucrezia*, was cast as the boxer, and Brian Reece as a fire-eating Prussian Count, who agreed, under pressure, that he was frightened even of his horse, and wouldn't really hurt a fly.

The show should have succeeded: Cochran, Ellis and A. P. H. all thought it would. It looked extremely handsome, with Cecil Beaton's admirable designs; Wendy Toye had again devised a polished and witty production. Tozzi and d'Atilli sang magnificently. But the show was a failure. A. P. H. blamed Cochran for casting d'Atilli, whose English was so poor that the audience could not hear his words; Ellis thought Cochran should have cut the piece, which was too long; and everyone blamed the weather – the play opened in the middle of an unprecedented heat-wave: twelve weeks of broiling hot sun. *Tough at the Top*, A. P. H.'s thirteenth show, came off after five months. It was also Cochran's last show: he died, tragically, as the result of an appalling domestic tragedy: arthritic, he was unable to reach the tap of his bath to turn off a stream of boiling water, and no-one heard his cries.

Ellis' next show was without A. P. H.: he wrote the music and lyrics for

Pamela Charles tries to prevent her boy-friend, Wallas Eaton, destroying a somewhat indelicate portrait of her painted by a handsome young artist she admires. in *The Water Gipsies* (1955), Dora Bryan (l.) was a major reason for the show's success.

J. B. Fagan's *And So to Bed*, a play drawn from Pepys' diaries. It opened at the New Theatre in October 1951, and ran for over 300 performances, with Leslie Henson as Pepys, Betty Paul as Mrs Pepys, and the young Keith Michell as Charles II. Then, A. P. H. was in touch again – in 1953 he had written a musical version of his novel about life on the canals, *The Water Gipsies*, and it was produced at the Winter Garden Theatre in August 1955, with Pamela Charles and Dora Bryan as the two sisters, Jane and Lily. The plot was pure musical comedy: Jane, simple and naive, becomes the doting model of a Kensington painter, while her knowing sister Lily believes that all he wants is her body – and not just on canvas. In the end, the artist, recognising Jane's beautiful purity, leaves her, and she marries the bargee who was her childhood sweetheart.

Ellis wrote an enchanting and rather delightful score, encompassing both the simplicity of 'Peace and Quiet', sung as he sat on the canal bank by the veteran actor Ernest Butcher, and the rumbustious 'Why Should Spring have All the Roses?', a number for Doris Hare and Jerry Verno as a couple of elderly lovers. Dora Bryan had one show-stopping number. 'You Never Know with Men'; Laurie Payne as the bargee sang 'Castles and Hearts and Roses', a hymn to the canal long-boats with their brightly coloured decorations; Pamela Charles a nostalgic number of make-believe, 'When I'm Washing Up' – and also 'Little Boat', the very first lyric of A. P. H. that Ellis had ever set.

The show received only moderately good notices, but was popular with the public – it was a genuine musical comedy in the tradition of the old Daly's musicals. Alas, Dora Bryan had to leave the cast after seven months, and the piece was taken off. It was A. P. H.'s last musical. Vivian Ellis went on to write the incidental music for *The Sleeping Prince*, played by Laurence Olivier and Vivienne Leigh in Coronation year; and the score of *Half in Earnest*, an adaptation of Wilde's *The Importance of Being Earnest*, which opened the Belgrade Theatre, Coventry.

A. P. H. was certainly one of the best English librettists of his time. His wit perhaps lacked the hilarious punchiness of Coward's, but for consistency and adeptness he can scarcely be bettered. He was a delighted exponent of the kind of light verse which has now virtually vanished, and his technique enabled him to work freely with his composer. His targets were predictable: he was, to use a term he would have hated, 'a square'. He was pretty far to the right in politics, and as far to the right in art – he disliked the work of most modern poets, and all forms of modern art. But even his prejudices (and every satirist needs them) were amusingly expressed, as when he gave Lord Harkaway, in *Tantivy Towers*, a song about an exhibition of modern art:

Was Sheba, the Queen who made Solomon gape,
  A collection of parallel lines?
Was Juliet just an elliptical shape
  With a few geometrical signs?
  Paint peonies green
  And I see what you mean.
Paint eyes like an ostrich's eggs,
  But *is* it the case
  That the girls of our race
Have such very triangular legs?

Other rhymers, when they put their minds to it, could possibly produce lines as enjoyable; it is true, arguably, that A. P. H. was in the end not quite universal enough as a wit. Certainly someone like Geoffrey Dunn, A. P. H.'s follower as a translator of Offenbach, is quite as adept at producing a good line. But A. P. H. was perhaps the last man who was able to write the kind of lyrics he could best write, for the kind of show which on the whole has now ceased to be produced. And he was very good at his job. His collaboration with Vivian Ellis, especially in their best show, *Bless the Bride*, produced an operetta as good as anything the English musical theatre has seen since the War.

When I included some of Vivian Ellis's music in a recent B.B.C. Series I was pleased that it attracted more attention from listeners than the music of any other composer I'd mentioned, including Coward and Novello!

8
True Operettas

'This is so little pudding I can't eat it!' – DAME ETHEL SMYTH

No-one who takes his music seriously would think of placing the musical plays of Ivor Novello, Noël Coward, Vivian Ellis in serious competition with the best operettas of Léhar or Leo Fall, Kálmán or Oscar Straus – or even describe more than one or two of their works as more than flirting with the notion of 'operetta'. A few post-1900 English composers attempted to write serious operetta, however – only to be greeted on the whole with the disdain of impresarios and the almost complete neglect of the public. One of these composers, Dame Ethel Smyth, complained in 1928 that though 'England's sole original contribution to the musical wealth of the world since Purcell's day has been in the domain of light opera' (so much for Elgar!), there were no facilities at all in the country for cultivating a talent for that kind of composition. 'All you get', wrote Dame Ethel, 'is two performances; then a couple of years' pause; then three performances, followed by two more years' pause; and so on. To quote my own remark as a child to my astonished grandmother, "This is so little pudding I can't eat it." '

Thomas Dunhill, the composer of *Tantivy Towers*, felt much the same way: 'At the present time', he wrote 'our theatres are content to import trash from America or dullness from Vienna or, alternatively, to employ native writers, who are frankly purveyors rather than artists, to stir the jazz-pot and ladle out the poisonous fluids in a tepid state to more or less apathetic audiences.'

Well, one must take both those remarks with the pinch of salt usually called for when neglected artists of a serious turn of mind are talking about less serious artists who have been more successful in their own field. But there is still some justice in them. There was no theatre in London to which a composer of true operetta could turn for a production; the most likely was the Lyric, Hammersmith, where Nigel Playfair did from time to time make an effort in the direction of more ambitious musical plays. But he bore the resulting losses almost alone. And it is not as though some of the better-trained, more serious composers did not write work which was worthy of success in its own time, and indeed is worthy of revival in our's.

To start with Ethel Smyth: she was an extraordinary, vital and interesting woman – really, the best woman composer Britain had produced up to her time, whose great ambitions lay in opera. She had studied music in

Germany, and when she was forty-eight, in 1906, her opera *The Wreckers* – her major work – was produced in Leipzig, Prague, and London, where it met generally speaking with a less than enthusiastic reception. The pattern was set by His Majesty King Edward VII, who was cajoled to His Majesty's Theatre for a performance under Sir Thomas Beecham. Afterwards, the conductor took the opportunity of asking His Majesty's Secretary how the King had enjoyed the performance. 'I don't know, Sir Thomas', replied the Secretary. 'You don't know?' said the astonished conductor. 'No, Sir; except that he woke up towards the end, turned to me and said "Confound it, that's the third time that infernal din has 'roused me!" '

Poor Dame Ethel found that her music met with the same somnambulant reception throughout her whole lifetime – her most popular work, for other than musical reasons, was her 'March of the Women', composed for the suffragette movement, of which she was a prominent supporter. She was once seen, when temporarily imprisoned for her suffragette activities, leaning from a cell window conducting with a toothbrush as some of her fellow prisoners trod steadily around the exercise yard singing her march.

It was on January 28, 1916, that her first operetta, *The Boatswain's Mate,* was performed by the Beecham Opera Company at the Shaftesbury. She turned to a short story from W. W. Jacobs' collection of humorous short stories *Captains All* – because of its theme, which has to do with the efficiency of women being more than a match for the craft of men. She went off to Egypt to write the work, first preparing the libretto, keeping much of Jacobs' original and amusing dialogue and including in her first act some folk songs, linking them by the spoken lines. The piece sounded at first more like a ballad-opera than an original work. But then, in the second act, the music became continuous and more original. She started the work off with a short, gay overture, which included a quotation from her 'March of the Women', and on the way home from Egypt signed a contract for a production of the operetta at Frankfurt-am-Main. But war came and prevented that – so it was left to Beecham to give the first performance in London.

The Boatswain's Mate has deserved the few revivals it has had: it was popular enough in 1916 to go straight into the repertory at the Old Vic, where Lilian Baylis's sterling work for opera was going on, and it was regularly performed there. Much of the music is gay and lively, and a great deal of the fun comes from Jacobs' original dialogue. It is true that Dame Ethel cheats by making the traditional Somerset folk-song 'Lord Rendal' the

Dame Ethel Smyth (1858-1944). Champion of women's rights, she was the first woman to write a full Mass. Her operettas *Entente Cordiale* and *The Boatswain's Mate* are full of her incomparable zest for life.

centre-piece of the first act, and indeed of the whole operetta; it is a lovely melody which towers over her own original contributions (though it might be alleged that she did not improve it by the idiosyncratic harmonisation she imposed upon it).

Ethel Smyth's second operetta came in 1925, and is perhaps more thoroughly an operetta than *The Boatswain's Mate. Entente Cordiale* is a farce arising from a British soldier's imperfect understanding of the French language – apparently the theme was suggested to the composer over dinner one evening by Oscar Wilde's beloved friend and counsellor, Robert Ross. Though it is in a sense demi-Sullivan, it has much more charm than *The Boatswain's Mate,* and it is sad that it never seems to have had more than a couple of performances at the Royal College of Music – amounting only to dress-rehearsals.

Gustav Holst, the composer best-known for *The Planets,* made several attempts at the operetta form – the first as early as 1892, when he was only eighteen and wrote *Lansdowne Castle* for the Cotswold Choral Society, of which he was conductor. It received only one production, at the Corn Exchange, Cheltenham. It is modelled on Sullivan, but has a number of ingratiating tunes, and was on the whole a success – though the provincial audience was shocked when Holst used a quotation from a Church chant as a magic incantation!

A few years later, after studying at the Royal College of Music, Holst wrote another little opera, *The Idea* (for the pupils of a school at Barnes, where he was by then music master). But it was in 1923 that his operetta *The Perfect Fool* was produced. He had begun to write it in the Middle East, in 1918-19, where he was organising concerts for British troops awaiting demobilisation after the end of the First World War. It is an ambitious piece, ambitious enough perhaps to be called a comic opera, but musically sufficiently lightweight to be more accurately described as operetta. It begins with a ballet. in which the spirts of Earth, Air, Fire and Water are summoned by a Wizard who orders a magic cup which will enable him to cast spells. The cup appears, and from it he gives a drink to a simple-minded young man who appears on the scene accompanied by his mother. The Fool drinks, and is instantly made irresistible to the local Princess, who falls in love with him. But when she asks him if he loves her, he answers – with the only word he utters during the entire piece – 'No', and falls asleep with simple boredom as the curtain falls.

The libretto of *The Perfect Fool* is a considerable mess, and a great barrier between the operetta and the audience, which showed signs at the first performance of not knowing what was going on. Inexperience of stagecraft meant that Holst missed several good dramatic opportunities, though occasionally his pastiches of other composers (mainly Verdi and Wagner) provide some good comic moments – as when the Wagnerian Traveller courts the Princess, and is rejected with the words 'But Sir, I think we have heard this before!' to the music of Siegfried's horn-call. *The Perfect Fool* has occasionally been revived, but could not be called a success.

Cecil Armstrong Gibbs had considerably more success with his operettas. On the staff of the Royal College of Music, he had composed some very beautiful settings of poetry, as well as some chamber music, before embarking on his first operetta, *The Blue Peter,* written to a libretto by A. P. Herbert. It had only four characters, was good-humoured and simply enjoyable. Like *Entente Cordiale,* it unfortunately only received one performance at the Royal College, and made no mark in the world.

With *Midsummer Madness,* produced in 1924, when Gibbs was thirty-five, he had more success. Written to a libretto by Clifford Bax (the dramatist whose romantic straight play *The Rose Without a Thorn* was to be his best piece), this was a full-length operetta, produced at the Lyric, Hammersmith. Again there were only four characters – two men and two women who met in a garden of a Somerset inn, and began to act a play (called *Midsummer Madness*) which had been rejected by the London managements. Involving Harlequin, Columbine and Pantaloon, it had the hackneyed theme of a young man who could not choose between two beautiful women – played by Marjorie Dixon and Marie Tempest. Approaching sixty, the latter was still absolutely enchanting: 'Her exquisite art made the rather clumsy dialogue as light as bubbles', one critic remarked.

Certainly the dialogue has its faults; but it is at all events craftsmanlike – neat and skilful – and if the piece begins in a rather chilling dampness and clouds over again towards the end, at least the middle act is played in an atmosphere of bright and cheerful warmth, and Gibbs neatly knits together musical sketches in various styles – ballad, Tudor Madrigal, and what *The Times* critic called 'filthy modernisms' – so that there are few dull moments. 'Put Down Your Tray', and 'Come, Will You Dance Me a Measure' are as delightful as anything in Sullivan, whom Gibbs evidently admired.

Talking of charm, one turns instinctively to Martin Shaw's *Mr Pepys,* which appeared at the Everyman Theatre in Hampstead on February 11, 1926. Shaw, who was organist at several London churches during his lifetime (notably at St Mary's, Primrose Hill), had an intense interest in English folk-song, and it is not surprising that when he turned to writing an operetta about that most English of characters, Samuel Pepys, he should have delighted in using the ballad-opera form.

Originally, in ballad-opera, words were fitted to already popular music – the most famous example is of course *The Beggar's Opera.* In this case, J. B. Fagan wrote a good book – not quite a play, not quite an operatic libretto, more a sort of genial charade; and while Shaw's tunes are certainly reminiscent of *The Beggar's Opera* and of Sullivan, they also have plenty of originality and a very great deal of charm, and were enchantingly orchestrated for a tiny band. One of the numbers had a considerable success, in a small way:

> You lov'd me once, I know.
> I did but turn my head
> And all your wits were fled –
> But that was long ago . . .

Frederick Ranalow played Pepys, Margot Sieveking Mrs Pepys, and Isabel Jeans Nell Gwyn; but though at the first performance there were encores of every number, the public preferred revivals of Gilbert and Sullivan, and *Mr Pepys* did not take.

Walter Leigh wrote two operettas, *The Pride of the Regiment* and *Jolly Roger*, which were both presented in the West End. Leigh was a serious composer whose career was to be sadly cut short by his death in action in Libya during the Second World War, at the age of thirty-seven. He had studied at Cambridge, and in Berlin under Hindemith, wrote a considerable amount of piano music, some songs, and some jazz. In 1932 when he was twenty-seven he collaborated with V. Clinton Baddeley, a contemporary, to produce *The Pride of the Regiment*.

Gervase Hughes, in his book *Composers of Operetta*, accuses the composer and his librettist of 'courting cheap popularity by introducing a catchy "theme-song" ("Love Calls as No-One Supposes")'. It is true that this melodious waltz-song (sung by Trefor Jones and Kathlyn Hilliard) was the hit of the first night; whether that cheapened the piece is doubtful – it aimed, after all, at being an entertainment rather than a great and intense artistic experience. It was set in the 1850s, with whiskered heroes of the Crimea, crinolined ladies given to the vapours, and Clinton Baddeley himself as General Sir Joshua Blazes, K.C.B., father of the heroine, Millicent Blazes. Mr Baddeley was apparently somewhat hampered by his invariable habit of singing out of tune, and the plot, in which the heroine married the hero after he had dogged the villain to the Crimea and come back thinly disguised as a gipsy, was less than convincing. But there is no doubt that a good time was had by all, or that the waltz-theme, together with other numbers ('The Miller's Daughter' and 'Month of May' – a song and dance for a chorus of ladies) were well received.

Leigh and Clinton Baddeley collaborated again in 1933 on *Jolly Roger*, which was produced at the Savoy in March with George Robey as Bold Ben Blister. Once more, there was nothing much of a plot; but the music was vital, and varied from a love duet for two elderly lovers ('Sweet William') to a rumbustious chorus for pirates ('Battery, Arson, Rape and Slaughter'). There were also a couple of good comic songs for the great clown, Robey, ('As You Might Say', a sort of slow patter song, and 'Romance', in which he was adventurous with castanets). Victor Orsini played the hero, a young man with an infinite capacity for getting himself arrested in every act, when not singing impassioned love-songs, and the music was generally considered to be worthy of the Savoy.

During the same decade, Arthur Benjamin, who had been born in Brisbane but received his musical education at the Royal College, was working on two operettas. The first, *The Devil Take Her,* was produced at the College in December 1931, with Trefor Jones as a poet whose wife is dumb. Receiving great inspiration from her silent beauty, the poet longs nevertheless for her to speak; but when she does, she is revealed as a termagant.

The libretto (by Alan Collard) is well constructed, and the score adroit, with a great deal of vigorous and lively characterisation. Sir Thomas Beecham conducted its first performance, and patted Benjamin approvingly on the back at the final curtain. But all the same, there could be no chance of the piece having a popular success: if Leigh 'courted popularity' by introducing a good tune into *The Pride of the Regiment,* no-one could accuse Benjamin of pandering to popular taste in *The Devil Take Her:* even the drinking song for an inebriated doctor was far too 'advanced' for his audience.

His second operetta, *Prima Donna,* though written in 1933, was not produced until February 1949, when the London Opera Club performed it with the composer conducting. This is about an amorous old man, his impecunious nephew, and two rival sopranos; there is a lot of accompanied recitative, some ballads, some parody of operatic conventions, some concerted ensembles, and a florid aria accompanied by the traditional flute. The ensembles are clever and witty, and there is a happy patter-song, as well as an ingenious duet in which two women singing in canon attempt to persuade the drunk old man that they are only one soprano. The piece had only the mildest critical success.

After a series of operettas which were only moderately successful, it is pleasant to turn to a piece which, though it has limitations, is still occasionally revived. It came from the pen of a substantial and successful major composer, Ralph Vaughan Williams, who by 1936 had already won a reputation as a symphonist, and as the composer of accomplished and popular works such the *Fantasia on a Theme of Tallis* and *The Lark Ascending*. There was some surprise when it was learned that, at the age of sixty-four, Vaughan Williams had written what was in fact a three-act operetta, though he described it as 'a romantic extravaganza'. But was it really so surprising that the composer of such delightful light music as the ballet score *Old King Cole* or the incidental music to *The Wasps* should wish to write a comic opera?

The Poisoned Kiss tells the story of a magician, Dipsacus, (all the characters have botanical names), jilted in his youth by an Empress, and in revenge planning the death of her son Amaryllus. The magician brings up his daughter on a diet of poison, and plans that when the two meet, her first kiss

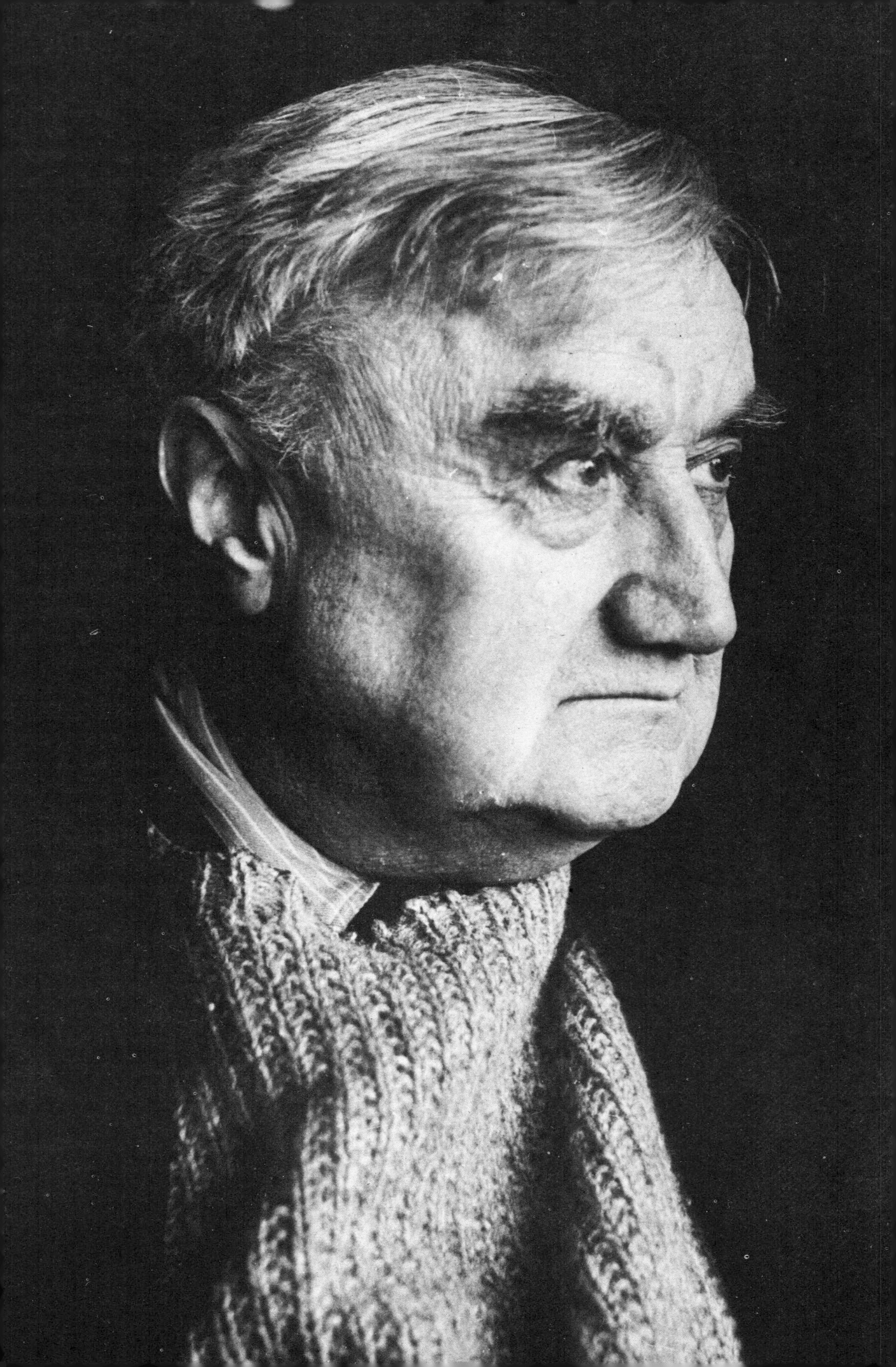

shall kill the Prince. But the Empress has meanwhile been bringing up her son on an antidote to the poison, and the plot fails – though in any event the operetta ends with a reconciliation and marriage of the magician and the empress. The libretto was by Evelyn Sharp, the sister of the folk-song collector Cecil Sharp; but Vaughan Williams took a masterful interest in it, and was constantly interfering with and altering it – not, it must be said, to its improvement. While critics have always condemned the libretto, and blamed it for the less than complete success of the work, this is really not entirely fair on Miss Sharp, whose work was again and again altered by the composer.

The operetta was written in 1929, but it was not until 1936 that it was produced – by the Cambridge University Musical Society, at the Cambridge Arts Theatre. With its jolly patter-songs, its syncopated waltzes, its Sullivan-influenced duet 'There Grew a Little Flow'r', and its satirical ensemble 'Today When All the World Behaves', it captivated its Cambridge audiences, and the critics on the whole liked the music when they heard it both there and a few days later at Sadler's Wells, when the composer conducted it. Richard Capell, in *The Daily Telegraph*, wrote: 'To enumerate the good things in the score would be to speak of every piece. Even the trio of hobgoblins disguised as newspaper interviewers turns out a capital piece of music . . . No more lovely song is in the work than the third act "Love Breaks All Rules". . .' Other critics wondered at the way in which Vaughan Williams had subdued his profound interest in folk-music, and could write such lilting tunes.

There have been many performances of *The Poisoned Kiss* by school operatic societies, though as far as we can discover, no full-scale professional production. Opera companies seem somewhat to have shared the attitude of the B.B.C., who declined the offer to broadcast the first London performance forty years ago. The failure of the composer's serious opera, *Pilgrim's Progress,* and the comparative failure of his other operas, may have helped to prompt the neglect of a very accessible and charming operetta which would certainly bear revival.

Two minor operettas, Anthony Hopkins' *Three's Company* and Lennox Berkeley's *A Dinner Engagement,* were performed during the fifties. *Three's Company* was given by Hopkins' own Intimate Opera Company in November 1953 at the Guildhall School of Music; a clever piece, it was compared at the time to a first-class highbrow revue, with its musical wit and ingenuity (there was the musico-dramatic use of the typewriter, for

Ralph Vaughan Williams (1872-1958), a symphonist who also wrote many works for the voice, including *The Pilgrim's Progress* and *Hugh the Drover*. His *The Poisoned Kiss* is an unjustly neglected operetta.

instance). The piece was produced by Eric Shilling, subsequently a stalwart of the National Opera Company.

Lennox Berkeley's *A Dinner Engagement* came out in 1954, given at Sadler's Wells by the English Opera Group. The libretto was by the accomplished stage- and screen-writer Paul Dehn, and is witty and assured; Berkeley rose to every opportunity with extremely singable and happily unpredictable melody. This, too, is a piece one could wish to hear again.

The English Opera Group, of course, specialised in the operas of Benjamin Britten; but it was not until 1976 that they had the opportunity to present his only assured operetta, *Paul Bunyan*. For years, the composer withheld this work from the public, and at the time it was written and first performed (at Brander Matthews Hall of the University of Columbia, New York, in May 1941) it disappointed both him and his librettists, W. H. Auden and Chester Kallman. Its broadcast by the B.B.C. in February 1976, followed by its presentation at the Aldeburgh Festival in June of the same year, proved it capable of sustaining interest, and no doubt it will from time to time be revived – in the autumn of 1976 it was toured throughout England by the English Music Theatre.

The libretto was the first to be written by the poet Auden and his friend Kallman – who went on to write distinguished libretti for other composers, among them Henze and Stravinsky – and they deliberately called *Paul Bunyan* 'an operetta in two acts and a prologue', a description accepted by the composer. In dealing with the legendary figure of Bunyan, with his mythical adventures and gigantic size, the composer and librettist presented producers with the difficult problem of staging a work the main protagonist of which 'appeared' only as a speaking voice from the sky (much like that of God in *Noye's Fludde*). There was also the difficulty of an opera without female voices, which was solved in part by writing-in a lumber-camp dog and two cats, sung by a coloratura soprano and two mezzo-sopranos.

The narrative ballads set between the scenes of the operetta – almost, as Auden said, like a solo Greek chorus – gave the poet the opportunity for adventurous passages of verse in the libretto, which is a lively and witty one, experimental but also 'popular' – as when Auden looks, if somewhat sideways, at conventional musical-comedy form:

> Swedish born and Swedish bred,
> Strong in the arm and dull in the head.
> Who can ever kill a Swede?
> His skull is very thick indeed.
> But once you get an idea in
> You'll never get it out again.

But the libretto also contains some of Auden's most magical lyrics – as in the song for the marriage of two of the characters, Hot Biscuit Slim and Miss Tiny, Bunyan's daughter:

The preacher shall dance at your marriage
  The steeple bend down to look
The pulpit and chairs shed suitable tears
  While the horses drawing your carriage
Sing agreeably agreeably agreeably of love.

The legend of Bunyan is simply told: how, in the American forests, where the young trees are bored and long for change, is born a boy with a shock of black hair, who gains 346lb every week, is as tall as the Empire State Building at eight, and whose stride measures 3.7 miles. Grown, he goes into the forest to make his fortune; works as a logger, gathering workers from all over the world, marries and has a daughter, and makes farmers of his men. The myth of the development of America is explored in accessible music and with delightful humour and a touch of satire – in, for instance, the character of Inkslinger, artist *manqué,* who ambles disconsolately through the piece, hating all country matters, and in the end is offered a post as Technical Adviser for a new, all-star lumber movie.

Britten once, in a broadcast interview, expressed a continued interest in operetta, and with his enormous talent for melody and humour, it is to be regretted that he did not at some later stage in his career return to the *genre.* His talent for immensely approachable music was fully apparent in such scores as *Let's Make an Opera, St Nicholas* and even *Albert Herring* – indeed only the scope of this latter piece persuades one to regard it as a comic opera rather than an operetta: there are scenes in it, notably the opening scene for the Vicar and his friends and Lady Billows, and the fête scene, which might be enjoyed by anyone who enjoys the more adventurous classics of light music, and certainly is more immediately appealing than some of the work we have spoken of in this chapter.

Right at the beginning of his career, William Walton, Britten's senior by eleven years, showed his ability for writing light music in the score of *Façade,* his music for (spoken) verses by Edith Sitwell. But it was not until 1967 that he wrote a work which may be called an operetta. His title for *The Bear* is 'an extravaganza', though happily Tchekhov, the author of the original short story, called it 'a vaudeville' (the title Mozart gave to *The Magic Flute!*). It was Britten's friend and companion, Peter Pears, who had suggested Tchekhov's story to Walton as a subject, and Paul Dehn wrote the verses added to Walton's own prose libretto.

The story of Madame Popov, mourning for her dead husband, first challenged to a duel and then courted by one of his creditors, is carried forward with enormous vigour, the music wickedly parodying Fauré, Richard Strauss and Puccini, and with a beautifully light texture accompanying the deft and witty words. First performed at the Aldeburgh Festival, and then handsomely recorded, it is a charming one-act piece, perhaps the finest example of genuine operetta of recent years – though necessarily musically too advanced to appeal to a contemporary audience on the scale of the great operettas of the nineteenth century. That kind of mass appeal is left to *Jesus Christ Superstar,* the 'rock opera' which we shall examine later.

9

Tunbridge, Waller, and Others

'The kind of thing the musical-comedy public likes best – complete vacuity of thought combined with lavish dispensation of everything else . . . ' – JAMES AGATE

The average, run-of-the-mill, entertaining but not outstanding musical comedies which held the stage in the thirties were exemplified by the productions of Jack Waller and Herbert Clayton. Between them, they presented in London a good many successful American productions, including *Mercenary Mary, Abie's Irish Rose, Hit the Deck,* and probably the best-known and most successful of all – *No, No, Nanette.* But quite apart from being a shrewd producer and businessman, Waller was also a composer, and in partnership with Joseph Tunbridge wrote a number of musicals which mostly starred one of the biggest comedy draws of the time, Bobby Howes.

Tunbridge was a quiet, unassuming man, shy and retiring, and it is difficult to discover much about his private life. Waller was more extrovert. He had been educated in Vienna, and started life giving twenty performances a week with Harry Reynolds' Minstrel Troupe, playing several musical instruments. Many years later, celebrating fifty years in show-business, he played with the composer Haydn Wood, for a private audience, Bach's double violin concerto in D major; and he was always prone, when being played a new score by a fellow-composer, to seize his violin and join in.

After appearing for some years on the halls, he formed the Seven Butterflies Concert Party, and toured all over the Empire with it; and it was in Australia that he presented his first play. For some years, his composing talent lay dormant: but he had always had an instinct for melody, and taught himself harmony and counterpoint and a certain amount of orchestration – and with Tunbridge (in a partnership so close that very considerable research sometimes fails to reveal who wrote which numbers) he composed, in 1931, a show called *For the Love of Mike,* which he presented in October of that year at the Saville, with Bobby Howes, Alfred Drayton, Syd Walker and Viola Tree.

Howes had, in this show, the number which virtually became his theme-song – Vivian Ellis' beautiful 'She's My Lovely', which had a wistful charm about it that was perfectly matched by Howes' own personality and his enormously attractive, individual light tenor voice. Born in Battersea in

1895, Howes had made his first stage appearance at fourteen, and, like Waller, toured the variety theatres and music-halls for years before making his first West End appearance in revue in 1923. He appeared in only one or two musicals before scoring his first great success in Vivian Ellis' *Mr Cinders* in 1929. From then on, he attracted a large personal following – mostly of women: small and endearing, with bright blue eyes and a broad grin, he contrived during the course of his shows to be bullied by a long succession of enormous and overpowering females (usually played by Vera Pearce), so that every woman in the audience longed to rescue and to mother him. His song from *Big Business* (again by Tunbridge and Waller) put it precisely:

> I've got a thing about you,
> Which makes me want to put a string about you
> And hold you tight.

For the Love of Mike was a moderate success, mainly on account of Howes and another comedian, Arthur Riscoe (they, one critic remarked, could have performed quite happily without a play at all). It had one particularly successful number, 'Got a Date With an Angel'.

In 1933, also at the Saville, came another Tunbridge and Waller musical – an adaptation of *Ambrose Applejohn's Adventure,* by Walter Hackett. *He Wanted Adventure* opened on March 29, and was much applauded for its rousing piratical chorus, its mutinies, stowaways and parades of beautiful captives. Waller shrewdly made a short (very short) version of the entire show, and recorded it on gramophone records. He was to do this for several of his shows, and the recordings provide a marvellously nostalgic record of the actual sound of the productions of the period. *He Wanted Adventure* played 152 performances at the Saville, and then made way for a new Tunbridge and Waller show, *Command Performance,* about a young actor who was ordered by the Chancellor of Baroc to woo the Princess of Vassau on behalf of his Prince, and did so well that the monarch abdicated in his favour! This was a show without Bobby Howes, and suffered accordingly. The score was only moderately happy – 'well enough in a conventional way', said *The Times;* and although Jeanne Aubert and Dennis King sang well, the plot was really too old-hat to be interesting ('Mr King played his part as though he had played it many times before', said *The Times;* adding 'as indeed he may have done'.)

Yes, Madam? which Tunbridge presented at the Hippodrome in September 1934, was another matter. Again, the score was nothing remarkable (the hit song, for what it is worth, was entitled 'Zip-tee-Tootle-tee-too-Pom-Pom'), but the play had a very sound plot based on a novel by K. R. G. Browne, and held the stage well. For once, most of the songs and dances actually had some relevance: a *colour ballet* came about, for instance, because the scene was set in a theatre where a rehearsal was taking place; and the ballet was danced in what the newspapers called 'modish frocks' because Binnie Hale played a character who had taken domestic service so that she would be entitled to a fortune, and this provided the excuse for her mistress and friends to parade themselves before her.

Binnie Hale had appeared with Bobby Howes in *Mr Cinders,* and their appearance together in *Yes, Madam?* (in which Mr Howes played a young man who had to take domestic service so that he would be entitled to a fortune!) pleased the public. She was an enchanting mercurial figure with a sweet, round face, and apart from having a clear and bright singing voice, danced with a quick charm that delighted her audiences: she was compared to a swallow, a will-o'-the-wisp and a sunbeam, and added a delicious humour to her movements. Her partnership with Howes was a memorable one. As to him – bullied yet again by Vera Peace, as the Madam in question, he pursued his own carefully light-hearted way through his part, and if nowadays his delivery of the dialogue has all the freshness and dramatic life of a reading from the *London Telephone Directory,* there is absolutely no denying the effect of his delivery of the many good numbers with which he was provided. *Yes, Madam?* held the stage for 300 performances and more.

Please Teacher, which followed it at the Hippodrome in October 1935, was quite as well received. Bobby Howes this time found himself stranded in a girls' school, and remained there for over 300 performances. Two songs from the show, 'You Give Me Ideas' and 'Mind How You Go Across the Road' had a small vogue. There was a much better number in *Big Business*, which opened at the Hippodrome in February 1937: 'An Hour Ago This Minute' was one of Tunbridge and Waller's very best songs, and went down well in a piece which had, it was complained, no beginning, middle or end, lurching between the business premises of Beauty-Cream Limited and the Magnapole Hotel, with a chorus dancing maniacally in drawing-room, office and roof-garden. Anyone in the audience who might have been mildly depressed by recent signs that musical comedies were beginning to have plots was thoroughly reassured, and enjoyed the Robin Hood Pageant, Bobby Howes' good burlesque (with Vera Pearce and Wylie Watson) of sentimental Negro songs, and the famous 'turn' in which a complex dance routine turned steadily into a series of catastrophic collisions. Wylie Watson had a personal success, appearing in various disguises including a giraffe and an upholstered chair.

The veteran musical comedy author, Guy Bolton, collaborated on the book of *Bobby Get Your Gun* with no fewer than four other authors. Produced in October 1938, it had a very tenuous story, set this time in Cambridge, with Bobby Howes as an undergraduate. There was a lot of de-bagging in the course of a search for a document proving his right to a peerage, and he and Wylie Watson disguised themselves as penguins, bloodthirsty gangsters, and other unusual characters. Bobby Howes was once more the real attraction. Ivor Brown, writing about the show, pointed out that 'the life and soul of the party, which flits from somewhere near Cambridge to somewhere near Cuba, is Mr Howes, who, like all good clowns, is a really good actor too, and will present you with a true image of anything from a colonel to a penguin, from a racing cox to a gangster terror. The best song is one of the gown- to-jazz-age, "Veni, Vedi, Swing It, Baby" – a modern classic indeed.' That modern classic did not survive, and *Bobby Get Your Gun* was the last notable Tunbridge and Waller show, though both lived on into the fifties.

A writer who worked steadily in the field of musical plays from the thirties right through until the fifties was Eric Maschwitz, who started life as Editor of *The Radio Times* under Sir John Reith, and for four years was Director of Variety for the B.B.C. His first musical, apart from *Goodnight, Vienna*, written for radio in 1932, and subsequently the first British musical 'talkie', was *Balalaika*, which started life in 1933 as *Gay Hussar* (a title which presumably would have a rather different promise today than it did then). The story was about Russian *émigrés* in Paris, and was based on an incident which had occurred when Maschwitz and some friends were in a Russian restaurant in Montmartre, and a young Russian killed himself nearby. It turned out that he had been a young man of title who formerly served in the Cossacks, and had fallen in love with a dancer from the Maryinsky, made his way back to St Petersburg to protect her when revolution came, but then discovered that her father was one of the communist leaders of the New Russia, and the sworn enemy of his class.

Maschwitz cobbled the story into a musical comedy plot, and George Posford – a young law student who had been writing incidental music for radio productions and for films – prepared the score. West End producers were unimpressed, and the script fell into the hands of Julian Wylie, 'the pantomime king', who produced it for a try-out in Manchester, in second-hand costumes and with settings from other shows. The first night was more or less disastrous (among other things, the leading man, Gene Gerrard, was almost boiled alive when a Russian bath in which he was sitting on-stage fused). *Gay Hussar* staggered around the provinces for a month or so, and then collapsed.

A year later, a South African financier was persuaded by Maschwitz's agent to put up the money for a West End production. Bernard Grun, a Czech composer who settled in London after being conductor at various theatres in Prague, Vienna and Berlin, and later wrote the music for over sixty films, worked on Posford's score, and a cast was assembled to be directed by Leontine Sagan, who had just worked on the production of *Glamorous Night*.

Re-named *Balalaika*, the show opened at the Adelphi in December 1936 – only an hour or so after Maschwitz and Posford had completed the new title-song, which became a hit. Highly sentimental, and produced at a time when the Abdication had underlined the difficulties of Royal love, it opened at precisely the right moment. Lit by a single candle, the narrator (played by Clifford Mollison) closed the piece with a speech that it is now difficult to believe was spoken with complete seriousness, even in a musical comedy:

> Well, *mes amis*, so ends our Russian New Year's Eve. Ah, those charming vanished New Year's Eves in St Petersburg . . . Is life perhaps a fairy tale? I wonder! The Count and the little ballet dancer . . . the beggar and the rich man's beautiful daughter . . . did it really happen – or was it just another story from the book? What do *you* think, my friends? I can't make up my mind!

The curtain fell in total silence, and for a moment Maschwitz thought the piece was a certain flop. Then suddenly everyone was on their feet cheering – the play had caught the imagination of the audience; and it ran for 570 performances, despite a few alarums and excursions when the Adelphi became unavailable, and a warrant was issued for the arrest of the financier who had backed the show, and had absconded leaving bills totalling three-quarters of a million pounds.

Maschwitz' second musical also had two names: it started out as *Paprika*, a piece with an Hungarian background and again written with George Posford and Bernard Grun. They worked on it together in Budapest, and it opened with a completely unknown Hungarian actress in the lead, right in the middle of the Munich crisis. It was received, on the first night, in almost total silence – except for wild applause at one moment, when someone sang a simple Victorian ballad. 'If that's all they can find to go mad about', said an actress to Maschwitz, 'you've got a flop.' And so they had. On the second night there were more people on-stage than in the audience.

Again, a South African came to the rescue, putting up the money to re-present the piece under a different name, in Manchester! Guy Bolton and Fred Thompson, probably the best musical-comedy writers available at the time, worked on the script, and *Paprika* became *Magyar Melody*, which ran for 105 performances at His Majesty's from January 1939. Its main distinction is that it was the first musical ever to be televised, live, from a theatre, though it became wildly popular, for some reason, with amateur operatic and dramatic societies.

Next, in 1942, came *Waltz Without End* – one of two musicals Maschwitz wrote to music by classical composers (in 1953, he was to write lyrics for Dvorak's music, for *Summer Song*). *Waltz Without End* features the life and music of Frederic Chopin, and is perhaps best forgotten – except that it provoked one of James Agate's most brilliant pieces. In *The Sunday Times* on October 4, 1942, he reported the trial of Mr Maschwitz, accused

> that on the 29th day of September, 1942, at the Cambridge Theatre, in a piece entitled *Waltz Without End*, he destroyed the reputation of Frederic Chopin. The Prosecution

says that to alter a composer's rhythms, key and tempi is to murder that composer. That to debase to blatant, mischievous and comic purpose part or parts of the B Flat Minor Scherzo and the finale of the B Minor Sonata, to divert from the piano to the voice some part or parts of the Third Etude, the E Flat Nocturne and the Waltz in D Flat, and to make such voices sing words that are the acme of tawdry nonsense, is to destroy the reputation of an exquisite composer . . .

Maschwitz was unrepentant, and indeed later claimed that the apogee of his career as a lyricist was to have set words to the *vivace* rhythm of the Scherzo from Dvorak's New World Symphony. (On the contrary, most people will remember him as the lyricist of 'These Foolish Things', and 'A Nightingale Sang in Berkeley Square').

His *Carissima*, mounted at the Palace in 1948, had music by the Austrian composer Hans May; *Belinda Fair* (a romance set in the eighteenth century about a girl who joined the army, impersonating a cousin too cowardly to volunteer) had music by Jack Strachey, who wrote the music of 'These Foolish Things'. *Carissima* opened in March 1949 at the Saville, and did not have a long run, though its music was heard from time to time on radio. (Incidentally, the first time most people in England heard the music of a new West End show was during the B.B.C. Light Programme's *Palm Court* on Sunday evenings, when the central spot was always devoted to a selection from the latest musical).

Zip Goes a Million, Maschwitz and Posford's best show, was based on an old American farce, *Brewster's Millions*, which had been a Broadway success in 1906. In the role of a young man who had to spend one million pounds in New York on New Year's Eve, the producers cast the comedian George Formby – the great ukelele-playing variety star who had made numerous film farces, but had never appeared in a musical or a straight play, and never before in the West End.

The piece was a success from its first night in October 1951. Besides Formby, greatly loved by his public (and deservedly so), there was Barbara Perry, a young American girl who brought the house down with a tap-dance rumba; and there were some good songs – notably 'Ordinary People', which became an instant hit, and 'It Takes No Time to Fall in Love'. Although after eight months Formby suffered a heart-attack (from which he was never fully to recover) and retired in favour of another comedian, Reg Dixon, the show went on to run for over 500 performances.

It was Maschwitz's last success: *Happy Holiday*, an indifferent musical version of Arnold Ridley's *The Ghost Train*, flopped badly in 1954. But he had

George Formby, a prolific film-maker: he and his ukelele starred in over twenty comedies. In 1951 he came out of retirement to appear in his first and only West End show, *Zip Goes a Million*. Tragically, he had to leave that success because of illness.

had a long and successful career, based perhaps more on professionalism and acumen than on any extraordinary talent.

Noel Gay – to return to a composer rather than a writer – was another matter. Between 1935 and 1948, he wrote eight musicals, and (like Tunbridge and Waller) wrote them for one star – Lupino Lane. Lane was a Londoner, and a very typical Londoner. He made his first stage appearance in 1896, at the age of four, on the same bill as the famous music-hall artiste Vesta Tilley, and gave his first real professional London performance at the London Pavilion when he was eleven. He had played in revue and musical comedy, in pantomime and on the halls, ever since – and had appeared in New York, too, in the Ziegfeld Follies.

Noel Gay's real name was Reginald Armitage, and he had been born in Wakefield in 1889 – where he showed musical promise at an early age, being appointed choirmaster at Wakefield Cathedral while still a boy. He had always meant – like many another composer of light music – to devote himself to the classics, and by eighteen was organist of St Anne's, Soho, and assistant organist of the Chapel Royal, St James's. But while he was at Cambridge, where he took his degree, he had discovered a talent for light music, studied Gilbert and Sullivan, and already found the secret of his success – which largely lay in the continual repetition of musical and verbal phrases. That may sound an oblique compliment: but in fact where that talent was used with flair and originality, it succeeded wildly – as in 'The Lambeth Walk', 'There's Something About a Soldier that is Fine, Fine, Fine', 'Around the Marble Arch', and 'The Fleet's in Port'.

He contributed a number of songs to revue – including 'All the King's Horses' for Cecily Courtneidge. In 1933 he wrote the score for Stanley Lupino's farce *That's a Pretty Thing*, and in 1935 wrote *Jack o'Diamonds*, for the Gaiety. But it was with *Love Laughs*, which opened at the Hippodrome in June 1935, that he found his feet. It was a simple little comedy on the old theme of the diamonds lent by a peer to an actress, and inevitably stolen (to be replaced by a set of duplicate diamonds, which were also stolen!) Laddie Cliff – who was to die two years later, in his mid-forties – appeared for the last time with Lupino, and with Syd Walker and the engaging Renée Houston. It was a happy show, and Gay wrote some good numbers for it, including 'Caravan of Dreams', and (for a chorus of convicts) 'O to be in Dartmoor Now that Spring is Here', the singing of which was interrupted in true musical-comedy fashion by the sudden apparition of a large chorus of girls in the prison cells.

Lupino Lane and Kim Kendall 'puckering up' in the long-running *Me and My Girl* (1937), which played for 1646 performances at the Victoria Palace. 'The Lambeth Walk' was its great hit.

LAMBETH
ARMS
COMPETITION
CAN YOUR
PERFORM
PRIZES
TONIGHT

Two years later came Gay's most famous musical – and one of the best-loved of the thirties and forties – *Me and My Girl*, which opened at the Victoria Palace in December 1937, and was revived there in August 1945, running in all for 1646 performances, which places it firmly in the top ten longest-running British musicals. George Graves appeared as an important baronet surrounded by peers and peeresses, all discomfited by the fact that the new Lord Hareford is a Cockney from Lambeth – Lupino Lane, of course. The show, as *The Times* pointed out, was in the old tradition of 'kind hearts in an uphill effort against coronets'; but Lupino Lane took the rather threadbare material and made it new, spicing it with innuendo and a splendid visual eye for comedy.

Gay's next show, *Wild Oats*, was presented at the Prince's in April 1938 – a really old-fashioned musical comedy in which (said *The Times*) 'the healthy and impatient burlesque of the music-hall persistently clears away the sad atmosphere of the nightclubs and the pretentious cynicism which is always apt to clog the gaiety of such occasions'. Nothing much survives of the score – nor of the score of *Present Arms*, which was staged at the Prince of Wales in May 1940, at the very low point of the war (it opened on the day the exiled Queen Wilhelmina arrived in London to take shelter at Buckingham Palace).

It reflected the times: the men were in khaki, the girls in French peasant dress; there was a scene in which a 'Lord Haw-Haw' broadcast propaganda. Max Wall did his by now famous eccentric dance, Billy Bennett (always billed as 'almost a gentleman') appeared 'in a bowler hat and a blazer which has a suspicious MCC look about it, and is not at all a gentleman'; the success of the evening was Phyllis Monkman singing 'Mademoiselle de France'.

La-di-da-di-da, which opened in March 1943, at the Victoria Palace, successfully pilloried and disposed of the old stolen-necklace plot, by dint of providing not one but a dozen cases of jewels, all of which were stolen, replaced, mislaid, confused, re-stolen . . . Lupino Lane appeared again, but was not in his best form, and the show kept coming to a dead stop for chorus set-pieces, or for a long cabaret featuring Nita and Noni, the acrobats. The show ran for 318 performances, and was replaced by *The Love Racket*, a sort of adult pantomime about three husbands who dreamed of fair women, with Arthur Askey, that beloved comedian, as a dame always disappearing through trapdoors. Valerie Tandy had a success with 'Homeward Bound', and Gay's 'Happy Days, Happy Months, Happy Years' was one of those numbers which, like the entire show, were 'happily detached from the war'.

Lupino Lane was right back on form in Gay's *Meet Me Victoria*, which opened at the Victoria Palace in April 1944. His impeccable comic mime was displayed in a legendary scene in which, as a railway porter engaged in a bogus marriage to a temperamental gorgon (played by Dorothy Ward), he tried to cope with serving dinner in a derailed Pullman carriage. And Gay's last show was *Bob's Your Uncle* (Saville, May 1948) – old-fashioned but funny, with the favourite Leslie Henson showing off his many comic faces, performing with great style in the inevitable drinking scene, and successfully putting off a proposal of marriage by pretending to be a villain. Valerie Tandy appeared again, and Gay worked with the lyricist Frank Eyton, who provided the lyrics for *Twenty to One* and *Crazy Days* for Billy Mayerl.

Billy Mayerl was a composer of whom personal details are scarce. He was an intensely shy and introverted man, who would never take part in any publicity for his musicals, and when in later years he became famous as a syncopated pianist, with many shows on radio and stage, he could barely bring himself to utter the words 'Good Night' at the end of his appearances. He was born in 1903, and entered Trinity College of Music at the early age of seven. When he was twelve, his talent as a pianist was such that he played Grieg's Piano Concerto at the Queen's Hall. But when his father, a professional musician, was forced to retire, he had to bring his serious studies to a premature end, and went to work as a pianist in an East End cinema orchestra for fifty shillings a week to help support his family. Within a few years he was playing with the famous Savoy Havana Band, in the early days of broadcasting, at £30 a week. He became well known as a radio pianist in the days of Savoy Hill, and the B.B.C.'s first music programmes, and he wrote many light piano pieces – 'Marigold' is probably the best known. At the end of his life, he was far better known for these, and as a pianist, than as the composer of musical-comedies. Yet in the thirties he wrote several quite successful full-length shows.

Nippy, which opened at the Prince Edward Theatre in October 1930, was a completely English show. The book was by Arthur Wimperis and Austin Melford – Wimperis was the author of an enormous number of musicals, Melford primarily an actor. Binnie Hale was the star, playing a waitress – the waitresses at Lyons' restaurants were in those days known as 'nippies'. A rather drunken young blade fell in love with her on boat-race night – but on the morning after, remembering, she rather doubted the purity of his motives. She was charming in the part: 'her acting keeps time with the conductor's baton, and while she acts and dances, she also sings', wrote a critic. She and Clifford Mollison sang Mayerl's 'I Feel So Safe With You', and 'It Must Be You', and the composer, as he so often did, recorded a piano reduction of the score.

Twenty to One, Mayerl's next show, had one instant hit – 'I've Never Felt Like This Before', and a good comic number, 'How d'You Like Your Eggs Fried?', of which Lupino Lane made the most. The show opened in November 1935 at the Coliseum, and was about an anti-gambling league which managed to hold its meetings at a fashionable racecourse, and to convert a prominent tipster (Lane), who with Clifford Mollison as the league's self-important president, provided some marvellous comedy. The production was beautifully dressed, proving (*The Times* remarked somewhat prissily) 'that frills and furbelows can hold their own upon the stage in an age addicted to scantier vesture.'

Twenty to One ran for 383 performances, and was revived at the Coliseum in February 1942 to run for another 408. Lupino Lane played the part of Bill Snibson 1025 times, and when the same character reappeared in *Me and My Girl*, went on to play him for another 1000 performances – which must be some sort of a record.

Over She Goes, 'a musical tantivy' which opened at the Saville in September 1936, a comedy in which a detective story had a flavour of huntin', shootin' and fishin', was written by Stanley Lupino, with music by Mayerl. Lupino appeared in the show with Laddie Cliff, his old partner, Syd Walker, Adèle Dixon and Richard Murdoch ('pale and polysyllabic'). Walker was especially popular, and had a good song about the police force, which he delivered in true music-hall style. Apart from this, 'I Breathe on Windows' was a success, and 'Mine's a Hopeless Case', a romantic number, was much recorded by various stars.

Mayerl's last two shows were less successful (*Over She Goes* had run for 248 performances). *Crazy Days* was again written by Lupino, with no particular story, but some nice 'business' for himself and the other actors – byplay with a straw hat, a duchess asphyxiated by a scent-spray . . . It played at the Saville from September 14, 1937. Two years later, in November 1939, came Mayerl's last musical, *Runaway Love*, 'a farce with musical interruptions' – one of them being the number 'Just Like a Cat with a Mouse'. George Gee and Eric Fawcett provided most of the fun, as two actors sharing the same bed in a Scots boarding-house.

Perhaps only two other productions of the thirties should be mentioned, and that for somewhat oblique reasons. In August 1934, *She Shall Have Music* appeared briefly at the Saville, the score provided by Christopher Fry, who after the Second World War was to become the focus of attention not as a composer but as the author of *The Lady's Not For Burning*, *A Sleep of Prisoners*, *Venus Observed* and other verse-plays – the centre of optimism for those who believed that a new age was dawning for poetic drama. Mr Fry only ever produced one other score – the incidental music for Peter Brook's *A Winter's Tale* at the Phoenix in 1951. *She Shall Have Music* was in no way exceptional, with its story of a crooner whose secretary changed identities with him to save him from the attentions of his fans. *The Times* awarded it 'a hopeful beta'.

By Appointment, produced at the New in October 1934, is memorable only because it starred the operatic soprano Maggie Teyte – who had, it is true, appeared in musical pieces before: in *Monsieur Beaucaire* at the Prince's in 1919, and in *A Little Dutch Girl* at the Lyric in 1920. But in those days, for an opera-singer to condescend to operetta or musical comedy was still, in England, unusual. Kennedy Russell wrote the score of *By Appointment*, the book was by Arthur Stanley, and Miss Teyte played Mrs Fitzherbert to the Prince Regent of Charles Mayhew. A genuine attempt at operetta, the score was mildly ambitious but lacked musical muscle; and the play itself was strangely constructed. There was a melting duet for Prinny and Mrs Fitz in the opening scene, in a card-room at Carlton House; but then Miss Teyte and Mr Mayhew disappeared for so long that the audience wondered whether they were ever to reappear. Meanwhile, there was a long scene in a shop kept by a beautiful exiled French Countess, during which there was a duet for an elderly coachman and a cook, 'An Old Man's Darling', which was perhaps the best number in the piece. However, the two leading players did eventually make their way back onto the stage, and Miss Teyte made the most of a series of songs – 'Dancing On Air', 'White Roses' and 'The Song is Sung' – which delighted the audience on the first night. But the piece did not run.

Apart from the revival of *The Dancing Years*, British musical comedy did not flourish during the Second World War; the real enthusiasm was for revue, and for certain 'straight' comedies. Perhaps two productions not mentioned in previous chapters should receive a passing glance: *Blossom Time*, which opened at the Lyric in March 1942, made use of the music of Schubert, set by Rodney Ackland in the narrative of the composer's life. With Richard Tauber – that magnificent tenor who, in the Austrian tradition, added triumphs in operetta to his triumphs in Mozart and Verdi – as Schubert, it ran for some time. And later in the War, in February 1943, Tauber wrote his own musical, *Old Chelsea*, with a Schubertian score.

In *Old Chelsea*, Tauber appeared as a professor of music too vague and absorbed in his studies to remember his debts or even which of several girls he was currently in love with. He was not the greatest actor in the world, tending to stride straight down to the footlights and hurl his numbers out into the auditorium – but with a voice of such charm and splendour that his audiences forgave him.

One musical comedy composer seems to bridge the gap between the thirties and the fifties – in style if not in fact. Harry Parr-Davies, born in Glamorganshire in 1914, wrote his first song at the age of twelve, when he was still at Neath Intermediate School. But then Sir Walford Davies – who did more to popularise classical music, through his famous broadcast talks, than perhaps any other single man – befriended and encouraged him, and by the time he was fourteen he had had six songs published, though his musical training was only marginal.

When Parr-Davis was eighteen, he went to London to make his

fortune – and was lucky enough to meet Gracie Fields, and to become her accompanist. For her, he wrote some excellent single numbers which she made famous – among them, 'Sing As You Go' and 'Wish Me Luck When You Wave Me Goodbye', 'An English Garden' and 'Smile When You Say Goodbye'. It was probably inevitable that sooner or later he should attempt a musical – and two in fact opened within a few weeks of each other. The first in order of composition was *The Knight Was Bold*, written with five other people, one of whom was its producer, Emile Littler. At that time, Littler had presented relatively few original musicals in London, but after *The Knight Was Bold* he was to go on to be the producer of a great number of successful British ones, including *Dear Miss Phoebe*, *Blue for a Boy*, and *Zip Goes a Million*.

Though *The Knight Was Bold* opened at the Piccadilly as late as July 1943, it was a musical of the pre-war type – even to the title of its best number: 'Whoopsy Diddly Dum de Dee'. Sonnie Hale saved the show from instant failure: hardly ever off the stage, and seldom slowing down to a walk, he provided some excellent comedy, and a dignified and charming Adèle Dixon played up to him marvellously.

When George Black heard the score, which was catchy and cheerful, he was sufficiently impressed to invite Parr-Davies to write the music for the stage production of *The Lisbon Story*, which opened at the Hippodrome in June 1943. Black's trust was amply justified, for apart from having generally pleasant music, *The Lisbon Story* also provided two smash hits – the ebullient 'Pedro the Fisherman', and the bewitching 'Some Day We shall Meet Again', one of the best romantic songs of its time. Harold Purcell's lyric caught perfectly the perrenial musical-comedy note of optimistic romance:

> Some day we shall meet again –
> I'll find you wherever you are.
> Dreams we'll mend at the journey's end
> And our hearts will follow their star.
> Some day, tho' the world is dark,
> The sunshine will guide through the rain –
> Love will last 'till the storm is past
> And we meet again.

The show followed the film technique even to flashbacks. The plot (also by Harold Purcell) was a pretty lame one, embellished with fashionable heroes and villains – British and Nazi secret agents. But there were some beautiful sets: a Portuguese village at the end of the first act, and a rehearsal of an operetta in an empty Paris theatre in the second. In the lead, Patricia Burke made a reputation overnight, and though most critics found that the evening occasionally dragged, the music was certainly acceptable.

Parr-Davies was far from lucky in his plots. *Jenny Jones* (opening at the Hippodrome in October 1944) was a *mélange* of anecdotes of Welsh village life, the main one of which was about a much-marrying man whose chief ambition was to father twenty children. Every now and then his increasing family was paraded for the delectation of the audience, which showed no spectacular interest; the piece was neither a comedy nor a musical comedy, and was much too small for the huge theatre. There were acres of flat dialogue, and the star, Baliol Holloway, predominantly a Shakespearean actor, played his part in an old-actorish, Dickensian way, which no-one appreciated.

James Agate wrote of it in *The Sunday Times*: 'It is . . . richly endowed with the kind of thing the musical-comedy public likes best – complete vacuity of thought combined with lavish dispensation of everything else . . . The plot of *Jenny Jones* is a jumble of insensate, staggering imbecility . . . anybody with any sense of the theatre would have cut nine-tenths of the play and entertained grave doubts about retaining the remaining tenth.' The leading role went to Carole Lynne, who, Agate said, was pretty, but 'whose singing, however, appeared to know nothing between an ultimate pianissimo and a piercing shriek of which Euston had been jealous'. The score could not rescue such an evening, but helped it along with such numbers as 'My Wish', which enjoyed a short vogue, and 'Where the Blue Begins'.

Parr-Davies went, for his next plot, to no less a writer than Sir James Barrie, and attempted to make a musical out of the charming and now under-rated Napoleonic period piece *Quality Street* – a Jane Austenish story of two maiden ladies who think that love has passed them by until the dashing Army officer, Valentine Brown, falls in love with the younger of them. Christopher Hassall, Ivor Novello's librettist (who was also to write the libretto for Sir William Walton's opera *Troilus and Cressida*) collaborated, and the adaptation opened on October 13, 1950, at the Phoenix.

The trouble, this time, underlining the difficulty of getting the balance right in musical comedy, was that the original play was too good. Most of the critics, knowing the play, were distressed by the cuts and by the music's interruption of it. The public was a little happier, but even it instinctively noticed the crashing gear-changes as Mr Hassall introduced the cues for songs. The score of *Dear Miss Phoebe* was pleasant enough – always workmanlike and sometimes more – and the lyrics were shrewd and witty and sometimes evocatively charming. 'Living a Dream' made the best impression on the first night, but it was 'I Left My Heart in an English Garden' that became the most popular song from the show, sung in it by Peter Graves as Valentine to the sisters Carol Raye and Olga Lindo.

Dear Miss Phoebe was not Parr-Davies' only show to be produced during 1950. *Blue for a Boy*, indeed, hit the jackpot for him, running for 664 performances at His Majesty's. It was an entirely harmless light entertainment, with no number in it better than its pretty but unimpressive title-song, and it is now difficult to say exactly why it caught the public's attention – one remembers the posters, with their portrait of the amiable

Fred Emney sporting, unlikely enough, a baby's rompers, and it may indeed have been his outsize personality that brought the customers in, rather than Parr-Davies' insignificant score, and the book of Austin Melford (who had collaborated with Leslie Henson in several comedies, including *It's a Boy!* and *It's a Girl!*).

In March 1953, Parr-Davies' last show, *The Glorious Days*, opened at the Palace. It was a mere arranging job, for in the show Anna Neagle appeared as Nell of Old Drury, as the young and the old Queen Victorias, and as herself – singing and dancing numbers from memorable twenties and thirties shows, against the background of a complex story in which a London taxi-driver, bomb-shocked, dreamed of the old days. Already, the times were passing Parr-Davies by: had he been born fifty years earlier, he might have been another Paul Rubens. As it was, he died – of the effect of heavy drinking on a gastric ulcer – in 1955.

Cage Me a Peacock remains to be considered from the forties. The novels of Noel Langley had something of a vogue at that time, being considered, among other things, enjoyably 'naughty' without being too permissively offensive, and Peter Bull spent his gratuity in mounting a musical version of one of them, with music by Norman Smith. This original version starred a music-hall singer called Phyllis Robins, who had had the remarkable distinction of recording, just before the war, a version of 'Smoke Gets in Your Eyes' which became Hitler's favourite gramophone record.

Poor Mr Bull lost all his savings in touring his production of *Cage Me a Peacock*, and waiting fruitlessly for a London theatre to become available. Eventually, the show collapsed, and was revived in June 1948, with an entirely new score by Eve Lynd, at the Strand, with Yolande Donlan as the Roman wanton sent off to exile in cold Britain, where there was much opportunity for fun of a rather obvious sort: modern slang in the mouths of ancient Romans; the appearance of an ancient Briton with a monocle and Civil Service manners. Though prettily designed, the new production was considered by Langley to be a travesty of the original conception (it was, for one thing, highly 'camp'); and the public shared the author's opinion. The piece only had a short success.

The fifties brought two surprising successes – *The Boy Friend* and *Salad Days* – which will be considered in the next chapter; and there were half-a-dozen varied British musicals some of which repeated the old formula – like *Bet Your Life*, in 1952, in which Arthur Askey appeared as a bridegroom who, it was discovered, talked in his sleep, successfully naming all the winning horses in the following day's big races. Not unnaturally his bedroom was soon crammed with relatives and friends and crooks, to the discomfiture of his bride. Alan Melville, a witty and successful writer of revues, provided the book and lyrics, and Kenneth Leslie-Smith and Charles Zwar the music; but the show received a mixed reception on its first night, and failed to run.

Donald Swann, later to become well known in partnership with Michael Flanders in the last of the intimate revues, wrote the score of *Wild Thyme*, a charming undergraduatish musical as simple as *Salad Days* and with a great deal to be said for it. Philip Guard had devised a story of a famous singer passing through a London railway terminus one spring morning, and indulging her longing for freedom by taking off for the country with an attractive railway porter. After an idyllic day she returned of course to her impresario husband, while the porter found solace in the arms of a country maiden.

It was all determinedly reminiscent, but with much charm (mirrored in the settings provided by Ronald Searle, with – as one critic put it – 'recklessly idiotic birds and snails and kite-flying cows'). Betty Paul played the singer, and Denis Quilley the porter. The show opened in July 1955 at the Duke of York's, but none of the numbers (the best of them given to choruses of hikers and yokels) caught the public's attention.

Grab Me a Gondola, which opened in Hammersmith but transferred to the Lyric in November 1956, was another matter. In it, Denis Quilley found himself in for a very considerable run, although in a piece without the charm of *Wild Thyme*. Julian More and James Gilbert respectively wrote the book and score of a piece set at the Venice Film Festival. It involved Joan Heal as a platinum blonde film-star queening it among the starlets and princes and gossip columnists, while really yearning for something better, and in 'Cravin' for Avon' expressing her determination one day to play Portia. Miss Heal set her eyes on the best-looking columnist (Mr Quilley), but he was determinedly defended by his fiancée, a suburban girl who fought back and won. The music was described as 'boisterously pleasant', and the show did well.

There is no justice in the world of musical plays: it depends as much as any other area of the theatre on what is fashionable as well as what is good, and the most charming show of the fifties was a total failure at the box office. James Ferman and Peter Tranchell, while still undergraduates at Cambridge, obtained the permission of Max Beerbohm to make a musical play out of his satirical novel *Zuleika Dobson*, the story of a girl so beautiful that the whole of the university of Oxford eventually commits suicide for love of her. For once, the writer, Mr Ferman, was entirely faithful to the book (except for the provision of a happy ending), and much of Beerbohm's peerless dialogue was preserved. Mr Tranchell wrote happy pages of pastiche of Edwardian light music, and Osbert Lancaster provided an enchanting décor (he gave one of the Sheldonian Emperors Max's neat Edwardian moustache). The cast – headed by Mildred Mayne as Zuleika, David Morton as the Duke of Dorset, and Peter Woodthorpe as the dim Yorkshireman, Noaks – played with complete sincerity.

Unfortunately, the producers who took *Zuleika* to the Saville in April 1957 were not confident enough to invest sufficient capital in it, and for this and doubtless other reasons (Beerbohm has always been a minority taste), the piece failed, though one or two numbers, notably 'Seventeen Years From Now', seemed at first likely to catch on.

There is no better production with which to end consideration of the fifties than the one which opened at the Palace Theatre on May 5, 1959, and closed a few days later. This was the heyday of the gossip columnists, who in the popular newspapers poked and pried their way into the private life of public figures with a determination only matched by their scurrility. John Osborne, the author of *Look Back in Anger*, had suffered from them, and had had enough. He decided to attack them through the unlikely medium of a musical play, and with Christopher Whelan writing the score, did so in *The World of Paul Slickey* (a tilt at two columnists in particular, William Hickey and Paul Tanfield).

Unfortunately, a lack of discipline allowed Osborne to turn aside from his central target and lay about him in wild swinges at almost everyone in sight – the popular newspapers themselves and their owners, the aristocracy, three separate pairs of adulterers, and popular taste. Then he ended the piece by having two of his characters change their sex (for no other reason, it seems, than that such medical phenomena were at that moment fashionable). Later, Osborne was to dedicate the printed edition of *Paul Slickey* to the journalists he had attacked: 'In this bleak time when such men have never had it so good', he wrote, 'this entertainment is dedicated to their boredom, their incomprehension, their distaste. It would be a sad error to raise a smile from them.'

Unfortunately, the effect he hoped his work would have on the journalists, it also had on the general public. When *The World of Paul Slickey* opened in Bournemouth, a large number of people either walked out or slept like babes for most of the evening; and at the Palace, later, the author was booed on the first night not only by the gallery but even from the stalls – an almost unprecedented act in the fifties.

Re-reading the text does not indicate that any great injustice was done to it by its universally bad reception, though as might be expected from a writer of such brilliant, if variable, talents, there are some shrewd hits – as when the chorus declaims a series of parodies of popular newspaper headlines of the fifties: **COME OFF IT YOU INTELLECTUALS; WHAT ON EARTH ARE THEY ANGRY ABOUT?** (the papers delighted in attacking the 'angry young men' of whom Osborne was allegedly one); **I BELIEVE IN BRITAIN** and **LIFE IS QUITE MORBID ENOUGH AS IT IS**. And at least *The World of Paul Slickey* indicated that no subject, no degree of 'tastelessness', if you like, was too extreme for use in a musical – an attitude which was to be mirrored, within the next twenty years, in shows from *Jesus Christ Superstar* to *The Rocky Horror Show*.

10

The Last Twenty Years

'I work best on a smaller scale, preferably when I know exactly what theatre and which actors I'm writing for.' – JULIEN SLADE

On the evening of April 14, 1953, a remarkable thing happened on the stage of the little Players' Theatre under the arches of Hungerford Bridge which carry the railway from Charing Cross Station out to the south-east. A show was performed which was unique in modern British theatrical history – a show which, though it was a pastiche of a musical of the twenties, was also at the same time a marvellous entertainment in its own right. It was later to run for over 2000 performances at Wyndham's, it was written by Sandy Wilson, and it was called *The Boy Friend*.

Sandy Wilson was only moderately well known in 1953 – as the author of sketches, music and lyrics for revue, and of the lyrics for a not very good musical (the score was by Geoffrey Wright) called *Caprice*. This was produced by Jack Waller, and conducted by his old collaborator, Joe Tunbridge. They were no longer in the first, or even second flush of youth, and the show opened and closed in Birmingham with inordinate rapidity.

It was not long after that unfortunate experience that Wilson was asked to write a piece for the Players' Theatre. The Players is a strange and fascinating institution – a club theatre specialising in nostalgia, which for most of the time presents evenings of music-hall, but every now and then commissions new short musicals which occupy two-thirds of the evening, and are introduced by half an hour of variety. The whole show, it was suggested, should run for about an hour, and Wilson decided that as a mark of respect to Richard Rodgers and Lorenz Hart – whom he revered as perhaps the best writers of musical comedy ever – he would call the show *The Boy Friend* (one of their best musicals had been *The Girl Friend*). Everyone was determined that it should be a genuine twenties show. The author was particularly fortunate that he had as director Vida Hope, who shared his feelings about *The Boy Friend* – that it was not a re-hash of anything, but 'a beautiful new show which they were rehearsing for the first time in 1926'.

Enormous care was taken about costumes, hair-dressing and make-up – false eye-lashes, for instance, were not allowed: hot-black was used; and Jimmy Thompson, one of the cast, discovered an old book on stage make-up, and from it copied the make-up advised for a juvenile lead of the period, 'with little red dots at the corners of the eyes and a touch of rouge on the chin and the ear-lobes, and arched eyebrows'. Fred Stone, one of the Players' best-known chairmen, had been in the choruses of several twenties musicals, and having been cast as the heroine's father in *The Boy Friend*, was able to give advice on stage movement, entrances and exits, and so on. The result was a show full of affection for its period, not guying it or sending it up, but observing it with loving affection. The audiences from the first night were infected with the cast's pleasure, and when after some difficulty – it had, for instance, to be considerably lengthened – it was produced in a conventional West End theatre, it ran until it seemed unlikely ever to stop, with Anne Rogers as the Girl who has invented a mythical Boy Friend in order to shake off unsuitable suitors.

The scene was impeccably 'twenties' – a young ladies' finishing school in Nice – and so was the plot, full of unlikely coincidences, carefully orchestrated misapprehensions, and with a messenger-boy who falls in love with the girl, and turns out of course to be a little more than a messenger-boy. Almost every number in the show was a winner: 'A Room in Bloomsbury', 'It's Never Too Late to Fall in Love' (in which Maria Charles and John Rutland had a special success), 'Won't You Charleston with Me'?, 'Fancy Forgetting', and of course 'I Could be Happy with You'.

Sandy Wilson faced considerable difficulty in continuing his career after the success of *The Boy Friend*. His first show to open after it, though before it reached the West End, was *The Buccaneer*, about an old-fashioned boys' magazine threatened with a take-over by an American tycoon who wants to turn it into a horror-comic. It opened at the New Watergate in September 1953, and later briefly appeared at the Lyric, Hammersmith, in 1955, in a substantially new production. But it never seemed to stand much of a chance of success, despite the good notices attracted by Kenneth Williams (in his first substantial role in the West End) as Montgomery Winterton, a wealthy infant prodigy.

The Times (whose drama critic had been the only one in town to see nothing in *The Boy Friend*) said of *The Buccaneer* that 'two or three of the songs allow one to see a little of what Mr Wilson may do when he has completed his experiments'. This patronising remark may or may not have spurred Wilson on to new experiments, but one remembers well with what surprise and mistrust one heard that he was thinking of making a musical of Ronald Firbank's novel *Valmouth*. The astonishing minor talent of Firbank seemed unlikely to survive transposition into another *genre*, but in fact Wilson (who had first come across his author during production of Firbank's one play, *The Princess Zoubaroff*) captured with astonishing facility the atmosphere of the novels, with their elegant depravity, febrile 'naughty' wit, quirky steeliness at the heart. *Valmouth* remains, in the view of many people, far and away Wilson's best work.

It opened at the Lyric, Hammersmith, in October 1958, again meticulously

Anne Rogers (fourth from l.) as Polly Browne in *The Boy Friend*, Sandy Wilson's affectionate homage to musical comedies of the 1920s, produced in 1954. Loving attention to detail helped to make the piece the riotous success it was.

and lovingly produced by Vida Hope, and with magnificent costumes and settings by Tony Walton. It transferred to the Saville, only to be withdrawn just as a prolonged run seemed within reach, because the theatre was committed to a production of Leonard Bernstein's *Candide* (so poorly directed and badly cast that it ran for only a few weeks).

When one considers that in 1958 the Lord Chamberlain still embraced the theatre in his wooly and stifling grasp, it is a wonder that *Valmouth* survived, with its dancing, lubricious cardinal, its scheming, randy Lady Parvula da Panzoust (played with the acme of smooth insinuation by Fenella Fielding), and a cast every one of whom obviously had sexual predilections as insistent as they were often unusual, despite the fact that several of them were centenarians. Even the innocent Niri-Esther, mourning for the absence of her lover, sang her entrancing little song 'I Loved a Man' while lying on her back supporting between her feet a large fish which was obviouslly phallic. And as for the show-stopping 'Niri-Esther' ('You're my friend, Jack, aren't you?' 'Yes, I am, Dick') done to a sly tap dance rhythm by Allan Edwards

and Aubrey Woods at the beginning of Act II – it was at that time the most overtly homosexual number ever to be seen in a musical, and brought the house down every evening.

But the musical was not simply an exhibition of 'camp' humour: it was also often extremely touching – the friendship between the centenarian countrywoman Mrs Tooke and the Negro masseuse Mrs Yajnavalkya, depicted in another of Sandy Wilson's enchanting numbers, 'I Will Miss You'; the gay little number for Denise Hurst as she celebrates the fact that she is soon to become 'The Lady of de Manor'; 'This is My Talking Day' for a nun released for twenty-four hours from her vow of silence; and the superb trio 'When All the Girls were Pretty', sung by Fenella Fielding, Betty Hardy and Barbara Couper, were all sheer delight.

Wilson's adaptation of the novel retained much of Firbank's inimitable dialogue, and he was spectacularly successful in maintaining the flavour in his own lyrics, deft and witty and immensely quotable. When the thunderstorms destroyed the world of Valmouth at the end of the evening, one felt a genuine pang of regret that such an enchanting, if cruel world, should indeed have existed only in the imagination. If one show of the fifties deserves revival – for it was well ahead of its time in all sorts of ways – *Valmouth* is it; it is a beautiful musical.

Subsequently, Sandy Wilson has failed to produce anything which has taken the public's attention to the same degree: neither *Divorce Me, Darling* (which again opened at the Players, and in 1965 moved to the Globe), or *His Monkey Wife* (produced at the Hampstead Theatre Club in 1971) were successful; but Mr Wilson's talent is too insistant for us to assume that his career is by any means over.

Long though the run which *The Boy Friend* enjoyed in the fifties, it was overtaken by another apparently unambitious show, which one looks back on with enormous nostalgia – Julian Slade's *Salad Days*, written as a sort of 'end of term' entertainment for the Bristol Old Vic, where Slade was engaged to provide incidental music. Transferred to the Vaudeville, where it opened in August 1954, it ran for 2283 performances, overtaking *The Boy Friend* by some 200 performances. Both pieces were subsequently revived: *The Boy Friend* in 1967, and *Salad Days* in 1976.

Julian Slade, born in 1930, was the son of a distinguished barrister. While his subsequent friend, Sandy Wilson (six years his senior), went to Harrow and Oxford, Slade went to Eton and Cambridge, and it was at the university that he decided to become an actor. But he was also a pianist, and John

Salad Days, Julian Slade's sentimental, nostalgic 1954 success, ran for 2283 performances and was revived in 1976. John Warner and Eleanor Drew appeared in the original production.

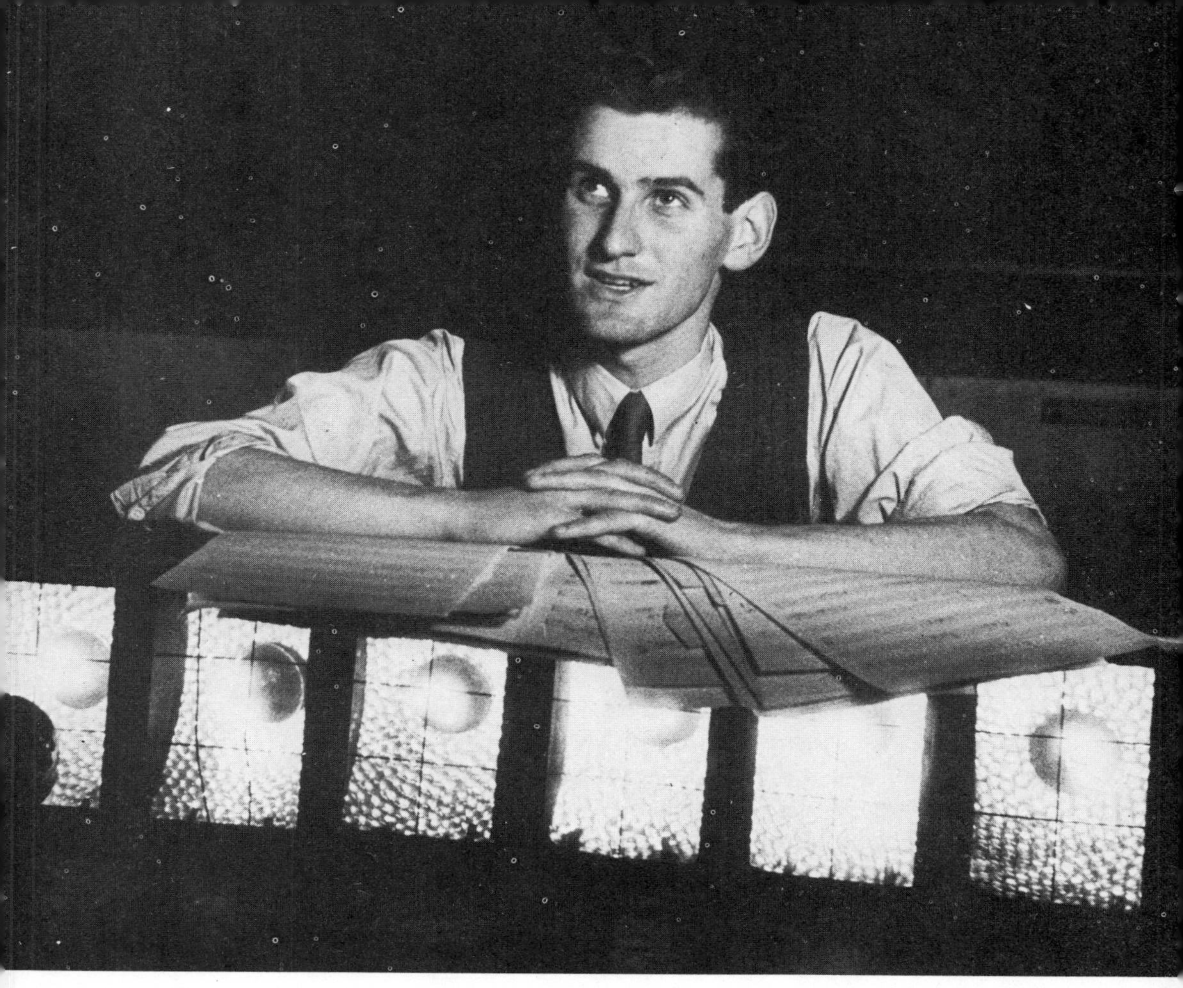

Julian Slade wrote his first musical (*Christmas at King Street*) in 1952, when he was 22. Two years later came *Salad Days*, and several other musicals have followed.

Barton, a contemporary, commissioned him to write an undergraduate musical for May Week; *Lady May* got no further than that – and neither did *Bang Goes the Meringue*, another undergraduate piece.

Meanwhile, Slade's ambition as an actor was not leading far: his best role had been Lady Macbeth, in the days when the Cambridge companies were still all-male. Joining the Bristol Old Vic, he still played small parts, and when volunteers were called for to provide a Christmas musical, he and the leading lady, Dorothy Reynolds, put their hands up. The result of their collaboration was *Christmas in King Street*. By the following year, they had worked on a score for *The Duenna*, Sheridan and Linley's comic opera, and Slade had become the Bristol Old Vic's musical director. For the following

Sandy Wilson's blockbusting success, *The Boy Friend*, came in 1953, and ran for five years at Wyndham's. *Valmouth* (1958), one of the most enchanting and amusing shows of its decade, has become a minor cult with its admirers.

Christmas they collaborated on another light-hearted musical, *Salad Days*, which they wrote in less than six weeks, and thought might run for three weeks in Bristol. It transferred, however, to the Vaudeville in August 1954, and Slade played the piano in the pit every night for the first eighteen months. The rest, as they say, is history, with such numbers as 'I Sit in the Sun', and 'We're Looking for a Piano' becoming little classics, with their fresh, youthful charm. If Slade is accused of writing 'pretty' tunes, that is perhaps not the least attractive talent in the world, though in the sixties and seventies it has proved a difficult talent to exercise, and he has never quite managed to recapture his first success.

With Miss Reynolds, he wrote *Free as Air* (which ran for a respectable 417 performances at the Savoy in 1957), and *Follow That Girl* (Vaudeville, 1959); then came *Hooray for Daisy* (Lyric, Hammersmith, 1960). Miss Reynolds deciding to concentrate on her acting career, Slade turned to Robin Millar and Alan Pryce-Jones for the book of his adaptation of *Vanity Fair*, produced at the Queen's in November 1962, and to Aubrey Woods for the adaptation of Pinero's *Trelawny of the 'Wells'*, which played briefly at Sadler's Wells in June 1972, and was transferred for a short run to the Prince of Wales.

Slade knows precisely where he stands; he once told Sheridan Morley in an interview: 'I'm never going to be the English Stephen Sondheim, any more than I was ever the English Rodgers and Hammerstein. I work best on a smaller scale, preferably when I know exactly what theatre and which actors I'm writing for.'

The third composer to dominate the light musical theatre in the fifties and sixties is Lionel Bart, who comes from a very different background to his colleagues Sandy Wilson and Julian Slade, and whose theatrical instinct (though not his melodic gift) is very different. Bart was born in 1930 in the East End – near the famous Petticoat Lane – and started life on a scholarship to a St Martin's Lane art school, in a job as a commercial artist, and playing the washboard in a skiffle group. After a spell in the R.A.F., he worked for a while in a printing works which he set up, and then became involved in amateur theatricals, where the actor Alfie Bass discovered and encouraged him.

But his theatrical start, professionally speaking, came at the Theatre Royal, Stratford East, which in the fifties was a hotbed of theatrical experiment conducted by Joan Littlewood, that astonishing woman of the theatre whose flair for success is equalled only by her flair for failure, and who for a time did more exciting work at Stratford East than was being done in the whole of the rest of the British Isles. It was she who encouraged Bart to write his first musical, *Fings Ain't What They Used t'Be*, which opened at Stratford in February 1959, was revived in December, and transferred to the Garrick in February of the following year, where it ran for over two years. Its

Fings Aint What They Used t'Be (1959) had music by Lionel Bart and a book by Frank Norman. Glynn Edwards and Miriam Karlin appeared in the re-presentation of the show at the Garrick in 1960: it had opened at Joan Littlewood's Stratford East.

ebullience, its forthright East End humour (aided no doubt by the disapproval of the Lord Chamberlain, who was still living in the age of *Chu Chin Chow*) gave it a *brio* which no other show of its time possessed – it was as far from *Salad Days* or *The Boy Friend* as jellied eels and green-pea liquor from smoked salmon and mayonnaise.

But apart from its mildly shocking quality, it has a wealth of splendid tunes, including the title-song. Taking advantage of its author Frank Norman's firsthand knowledge, it was set in the sleazy world of the London petty crooks. It consisted of a series of thumbnail sketches of low life – a sort of modern Mayhew – with razor kings gambling with marked cards, whores

and their pimps, a policeman happily accepting bribes, and a razor battle off-stage accompanied by a rousing chorus number, 'Carve-Up'.

The witty lyrics of *Lock Up Your Daughters*, the musical version of Fielding's *Rape Upon Rape* with which Sir Bernard Miles opened the Mermaid Theatre in May 1959, were written by Bart (the score was by Laurie Johnson); and he went on to produce his most successful show to date, *Oliver!*, which he adapted from Dickens' *Oliver Twist*, and which ran for 2618 performances at the New (from June 30, 1960) – not to mention 331 performances when it was revived in 1967 – making it the longest-running British musical ever, overtaken only by *The Black and White Minstrel Show* and *The Mousetrap* in any London theatre at any time.

The secret of the success of *Oliver!* is not difficult to fathom: Dickens' original story, with its marvellously strong story-line and its familiarity to most of the audience, was as good a starting-point as any. Then there was the excellence of the score (and not only in its hit numbers such as 'As Long as You Need Me', sung with moving passion by Georgia Brown, whose Nancy was one of the piece's two leading performances; the orphans' 'Food, Wonderful Food'; Fagin's 'Gotta Pick a Pocket or Two', and the rest, but even the minor numbers). There was a first-rate cast, at the centre of which cavorted and leered the magnificent Fagin of Ron Moody, an actor apparently born for the part, and giving in it a virtuoso performance happily preserved in the film of the show – the best British musical film yet made – and unlikely to be forgotten by anyone who saw it.

Two years later, Bart's new musical was ready for production, and opened at the Adelphi on May 8, 1962. Based on his own memory of the effects of the war in his own East End, it was called *Blitz*. Visiting it, Noël Coward remarked that it was as loud as the real thing and twice as long; the official critics were not much kinder. None of the numbers in the score caught on with the public – though there were some good ones, especially for the children, whose marching song 'We're Off to See the Country' as they trooped down to the station to be evacuated, was touching and memorable. The major effect of the evening was made by the enormously complex set built by Sean Kenny, then the most adventurous and fashionable designer working in the theatre. The beams and constructions with which the stage was filled seemed to march and waltz and move with the piece, so that when one critic alleged that he had come out 'whistling the scenery', one could only acknowledge that there was some truth in it. Mr Kenny now appears to have been striding down a blind alley, and just as his ludicrous set for

Vivienne Martin as Nancy in Lionel Bart's *Oliver!* sings 'Oom-pah-pah!' at The Three Cripples pub. *Oliver!*, which opened in 1960, remains the longest-running British musical.

Covent Garden's *Flying Dutchman* battled (and lost) with the music of Wagner, so his set for *Blitz* can now be said to have done little for Bart's conception. Still, *Blitz* ran for 567 performances, a run which the management of Daly's or the Gaiety would have been delighted with in the 1900s, if it was by the sixties almost the minimum necessary to any management coping with the enormously increased costs of production. Production costs were indeed to haunt Bart and his backers from *Blitz* onwards.

Maggie May, the book by the television playwright Alun Owen, and directed by Ted Kotcheff, then a television director, opened at the Adelphi in September 1964, and told the story of the archetypal dockside Liverpool whore – a prostitute ready to reform when her only lover, dismissed from the Navy, returns to become a docker. But he finds that he is being used to help transport arms to South America, and leaves Maggie to lead an unofficial strike, and then to kill himself while destroying the cargo his fellow-dockers are prepared to handle for extra pay.

Sean Kenny once again built a huge and ambitious set or series of sets – streets, warehouses, docks, a ferryboat and New Brighton fair-ground – and Rachel Roberts and Kenneth Haigh led the cast splendidly. After the curtain the old, bawdy Liverpool song was sent out into the auditorium:

> O dirty Maggie May
> They have taken her away –
> No more she'll walk down Lime Street after dark . . .

and there were scenes of enthusiasm which must have encouraged Bart to believe that he had a greater success than *Oliver!* all wrapped up. But the show ran for only 501 performances. And with *Twang!!*, his next musical, Bart was to discover, fatally, how hard a gamble the production of a large-scale musical had become. (It was a lesson taken to heart by theatre impresarios, too, and the production of a major musical has been a matter for extreme caution ever since.)

Twang!! was based on an entirely acceptable idea: it was to be a musical about Robin Hood and his Merry Men with, of course, Maid Marion and all the usual characters. The story of the production can scarcely be told by anyone not involved in it: rumours of intrigue and quarrel, betrayal and desertion, echoed around it from the beginning, and were fuelled when Joan Littlewood, the director, swept out not long before the first night of the provincial try-out.

At least some of the trouble lay with the book, which was written by Harvey Orkin, an American who had built a temporary reputation as a wit on the then popular television programme *That Was The Week That Was*. But Mr Orkin had not decided precisely what the show was to be about; the story line, *The Times* complained, was 'as clear as a tattered cobweb', and there seemed to be no single witty line, and not one good theatrical situation. Though visually there were compensations – Oliver Messel had designed the show with great flair, and entertaining contrasts – and though Paddy Stone's choreography was inventive – a scene around a gallows becoming a morris-dance around a maypole – though James Booth (Robin Hood) and Barbara Windsor (Maid Marion) gave enjoyable performances – Maid Marion being a happy nymphomaniac – the evening had a cardboard cut-out, cheaply comic pantomime atmosphere which nothing could dispel.

There were appalling notices on the morning after the first night at the Shaftesbury on December 20, 1965, and *Twang!!* was doomed. The death-blow was struck by the powerful ticket agency, Keith Prowse, which failed to take up the block bookings which could have supported the show. Bart gallantly signed sureties of £4000 a week for three weeks running, in an attempt to nurse the show; but it collapsed and closed, losing, it is estimated, something over £80,000 by the time all the bills were paid.

Something of Bart's enthusiasm for the *genre* seems to have been killed by the fiasco of *Twang!!*, for despite the enormous success of the film of *Oliver!*, he has so far failed to recover his old panache and tunefulness. The only show which looked promising was *Costa Packet*, produced at Stratford East in October 1972.

Costa Packet set out to satirise the all-in package holiday business, and Bart collaborated with Frank Norman, the author of *Fings*, and with Alan Klein. A tourist group on an excursion to Spain faced all the hazards – foreign cooking and insects, uncompleted hotels, lecherous local lads – while still asserting that life there was better than life in a rebuilt and soulless Walthamstow. The cast was excellent, headed by Avis Bunnage as an Edgebaston snob, and Joan Littlewood's production was inventive and full of life. But somehow none of the individual numbers was quite good enough, and the humour – the humour of the twopence-coloured comic postcard – seemed curiously dated. As a whole, it simply failed to work, and never reached the West End.

One turns, after these three major figures, to the clutch of other composers and writers who had successes during the sixties and seventies. David Heneker is certainly one of these. Somewhat surprisingly, he turns out to have been in the Army for over twenty years, a full Colonel who resigned his commission in 1937 in order to write music, and came to the fore with *Half a Sixpence*, the adaptation of H. G. Wells' *Kipps* which opened at the Cambridge on March 21, 1963, and ran for 678 performances with Tommy Steele in the title-role.

Heneker had worked on other shows before that – notably *Expresso Bongo* (in collaboration with Monty Norman, at the Saville in 1958), and *Make Me an*

Tommy Steele as Kipps in the wedding scene from David Heneker's *Half a Sixpence* (1963) kneels in front of Marti Webb, the bride. 'Flash Bang, Wallop (what a photograph)', sung in this scene, was a show-stopper.

Offer (at Stratford East and later in the West End, in 1959). But *Half a Sixpence*, though arguably not much to do with Wells, was the real break-through, no doubt due in part to Steele's gaiety and appeal, but certainly also to a bright and giving score, the show-stopper of which was 'Flash Bang Wallop', sung while a Victorian photographer was taking a wedding group. The title-song, too, became familiar.

If *Half a Sixpence* was a musical of the old, and by now thoroughly dated, style, *Charlie Girl* emerged triumphantly through an even thicker curtain of cobwebs to demonstrate that what the public wanted – what the public so often wants in its light entertainment – is an assurance that nothing has changed. It could have been written in 1920, with its typical musical-comedy story of the boyish daughter of a former show-girl now the mistress of a

Charlie Girl, which received abysmal reviews, went on to be a long-running success (1963). Left to right, Derek Nimmo, Hy Hazell, Anna Neagle, Christine Holmes, Joe Brown.

stately home. The story was really, in fact, like one of the old burlesques: Cinderella-up-to-date, with the ugly sisters reborn as two debs, Prince Charming as a vain American playboy, and Cinders mucking about in the garage in overalls, and eventually falling for Buttons, the Cockney boy who runs the estate for mother.

Anna Neagle played the ex-show girl, Joe Brown the neo-Buttons, and Derek Nimmo had one of his first really popular comic roles as a pools-tycoon now engaged as a butler. It was all very popular; but it must be said that the six authors who collaborated on *Charlie Girl* (including Hugh and Margaret Williams, the joint authors of many popular West End comedies) had taken immense trouble to ensure that no-one could possibly be offended by a single word in the piece; just as no ear could be struck by the faintest originality or discord in David Heneker's music. The critics described the result as 'pap'; everyone concerned smiled happily all the way to their respective banks.

For his next musical, Heneker turned to a 'classic' beloved of a great number of readers – the adventures of *Jorrocks*, Robert Surtees' fox-hunting man, with the comedian Jimmy Edwards in the title-role, and making a success of it, though no more like Surtees' Jorrocks than Tommy Steele had been like Wells' Kipps.

Leslie Bricusse has concentrated his talents most successfully in films – notably *Dr Doolittle*, *Goodbye Mr Chips* and *Scrooge*. But with Anthony Newley (the boy-star of the Alec Guinness film of *Oliver Twist* in the forties) he did write two prominent West End musicals.

It was in *Stop the World, I Want to Get Off* that Bricusse and Newley had their first success. It opened at the Queen's in July 1960, with a striking Sean Kenny set, and ran for 478 performances with Newley as a penniless boy who became a millionaire, peer and elder statesman, had many unwanted children by a great number of women of various nationalities, and ended up singing a pathetic song about his own selfishness and loneliness.

If it all sounds a little soft and gooey now, it was a major success at the time; but Newley's preoccupation with the 'Laugh, Clown, Laugh' syndrome had by the end of its run become too familiar to cut much ice when *The Good Old Bad Old Days* opened eleven years later.

The Good Old Bad Old Days, produced at the Prince of Wales on December 20, 1972, was a theatrical survey of man's history from Roman times to the present day, with Newley himself as a harmless waif who also appeared as the Devil. If that suggests some confusion, the impression is a correct one; the show was enormously complicated and muddled, though there were one or two good numbers such as 'The Fool who Dared to Dream' and 'The Good Things in Life', as well as the title-song.

'It's a sort of pantomime for adults', said Newley; but not one with sufficient punch to hold an audience of adults – even with such spectacular numbers as the Dixieland and Ziegfeld Follies set-pieces, each of which incidentally dissolved into war, in an attempt to make the same kind of point that *Oh What a Lovely War* had made at Wyndham's in 1963, using the traditional songs of 1914-18 (another brilliant conception which originated with Joan Littlewood and her team).

It was with *Pickwick*, a musical adaptation of Dickens' picaresque early novel, that Bricusse had his most substantial success so far – though he only wrote the lyrics for music by Cyril Ornadel. *Pickwick* was one of those shows which it is difficult now to believe could ever have failed, given the spirit of the original, successfully transferred to the stage by Wolf Mankowitz. There were admirable performances by a number of players, including Peter Bull

Mr Pickwick (Harry Secombe) is cross-examined by the masterful Sergeant Buzzfuzz (Peter Bull) in the 1963 production of *Pickwick* at the Saville.

and Julian Orchard. and the central figure – substantial in all senses – of Harry Secombe, who for years was not allowed to make an appearance on stage or screen without singing the theme-song from the play, 'If I Ruled the World'. His genial spirit would have carried a much less attractive piece than *Pickwick*, which had a long run at the Saville from July 1963.

The sixties had opened with another musical by the team which had produced *Grab Me a Gondola* – and most of the critics grudgingly allowed that anyone who had enjoyed the first show would enjoy *The Golden Touch*, which opened at the Piccadilly in May. (Alas, not enough of them did.) The new show dealt with the world of high finance, with a millionaire ship-owner attempting to take over a Greek island as a port for his merchant fleet. Unfortunately, on the island lives a hippy community of which his daughter is a leading figure. The millionaire sends a young adviser to persuade the community to leave: but, foreseeably, the young man is seduced by the daughter and her way of life – while the daughter and her followers begin to think that perhaps unlimited money has something to be said for it.

James Gilbert's music was loud and uncatchy, and the cast seemed to feel that noise equalled musicality. The imitation American dialogue was awful, and Paddy Stone's brilliant choreography (much influenced by *West Side Story*) and the dancing of Gary Cockrell, who had appeared in that show, could not save it. Interestingly, the décor was by the architect Sir Hugh Casson.

An unusual entertainment opened at the Strand in May 1961. *Belle*, with a book by Wolf Mankowitz and music and lyrics by Monty Norman, presented the story of Dr Crippen and Ethel le Neve as it might have been told by variety stars of the 1880s, and in the form of a music-hall ballad opera. The main pleasure of the evening was in the spirited impersonations of music-hall stars – by Jerry Desmonde (as George Lashwood), Davy Kaye (as Little Tich) and Nicolette Roeg (as Vesta Tilley). Crippen's wife, Belle, was seen as a mock music-hall star herself, whom he poisoned almost without meaning it. Virginia Vernon played Ethel le Neve, his mistress, and George Benson was magnificent as Crippen. But despite Monty Norman's pleasant tunes, the piece did not take.

Robert and Elizabeth, which opened in October 1964, at the Lyric, was the first British musical since *Pickwick* to enjoy a real success. It was based by Ronald Millar on Rudolf Besier's immensely popular play, *The Barretts of Wimpole Street*, which had often been revived. It told the story of the abduction of Elizabeth Barrett from her father's house by the young poet Robert Browning. The king-pin of the original play was the portrait of the obsessive, sexually repressed, tyrannical Mr Barrett (most familiar to audiences through the screen portrayal by Charles Laughton). In shortening the play, Millar substantially constricted that character, as well as altering the atmosphere by opening out the scene from the claustrophobic rooms in Wimpole Street to encompass a garden in which there could be dancing. Though John Clements gave a splendid performance as Mr Barrett, the role inevitably lost some conviction.

However, June Bronhill (then at the height of a popularity which began with a sparkling *Merry Widow* at Sadler's Wells) and Keith Michell were the young lovers, and Ron Grainer provided some excellent chorus-songs. While there was no single show-stopping number, there were some ambitious and occasionally distinctive songs (the quiet little waltz for the Barrett children, for instance). The piece deserved its good run.

In 1966, the strike of girls in a match factory in the East End of the 1880s was the subject of *The Matchgirls* (at the Globe in March) and of *Strike a Light* (at the Piccadilly in July). Inevitably, both productions covered the same ground. *The Matchgirls* was primarily a rather didactic piece, the curtain rising on a Hogarthian scene of thin, waif-like girls working in dreadful conditions, terrified of contracting 'phossy-jaw' – a phospherous infection. Bill Owen's script, while its heart was in the right place, was the script of an actor rather than a writer, and the dialogue was flat and uninspired, if not (as when he attempted to portray Annie Besant, the theosophist and revolutionary Socialist) embarrassing. As the evening wore on, it became more like a pantomime or a Victorian melodrama with music, than anything else. Tony Russell's music was cheerful and blowsy and entirely apt in such scenes as the hop-picking knees-up.

Strike a Light was much more theatrical: it made concessions which destroyed its pretensions, if it had any, to social history. The girls were all pretty and well-fed, and the strike-leader, played by Jeannie Carson without the fire and attack of Vivienne Martin in the same role in *The Matchgirls*, was even at one point heard to ask Mrs Besant to give her lessons in manners. But it was a better show, for all that, and a more professional score from Gordon Caleb made it a likely runner – though over a shorter course.

The Marie Lloyd Story, which played at the Theatre Royal, Stratford East, in November 1967, did not have to compete directly with *Sing a Rude Song*, which came to the Garrick three years later. But both dealt with the later life of the famous music-hall star. The Stratford show was written by Daniel Farson and Harry Moore, whose love of the music-hall resulted in spasmodically brilliant recreations of the atmosphere of the halls of the time – triumphantly bouncy acts ablaze with life before the public, and sleazy backstage gossip before and after.

Both plays covered the years during which the middle-aged star fell in love with a young Irish jockey and fought with the Purity Campaign. Forced to alter a line in one of her songs which went 'She sits among the cabbages and peas', she amended it to 'She sits among the cabbages and leeks'. She was arrested in the United States for 'moral turpitude', and, old before her time, finally collapsed on the stage of the Edmonton Empire.

Once more, Joan Littlewood fought with her authors, imposing on the piece some production effects which did not help it. Thus at Romano's a high-kicking chorus-girl competed with a belly-dancer, and there was an unprovoked free fight to add spurious 'liveliness' which destroyed the carefully-constructed atmosphere of the script. Norman Kaye's score managed to hold its own against the magnificent lilting tunes of the original music-hall songs, and Avis Bunnage gave a splendid performance as Marie Lloyd; but the play did not transfer to the West End.

That admirable Cockney comédienne, Barbara Windsor, was cast as Marie Lloyd in *Sing a Rude Song*, written by Caryl Brahms and Ned Sherrin, with music by Ron Grainer and Alan Bennett. On the first night, Marie's sister was in the house. Afterwards, she said: 'Miss Windsor did her best, worked very hard, and had lots of changes. The poor soul must have been exhausted at the finish – but I regret I cannot say she reminded me much of Marie.' The book was not as affectionate or as theatrical as Farson's and Moore's, and the composers crammed the show with far too many numbers, none of them memorable.

Nostalgia informed two more shows, both of which deserved success, and one of which attained it. Neville Coghill's 'translation' of *The Canterbury Tales* had brought Chaucer a large readership since its publication some years previously. In March, 1968, it reached the stage of the Phoenix, in a dramatisation by Martin Starkie, and with music by Richard Hill and John Hawkins, orchestrated largely for brass with a splendid mock-medieval sound.

The producers had obviously counted on the Lord Chamberlain's respect for the glories of Eng. Lit. to inhibit him from cutting a classic, and the bawdy and suggestiveness no doubt attracted some members of the audience. But the play deserved its long run on other grounds too – for its lightheartedness and its respect for the spirit of the original. Wilfred Brambell in particular had a great personal success with his pre-nuptial samba, but Nicky Henson (the son of that veteran of musical comedy, Leslie Henson) and C. Denier Warren were also memorably lively and amusing.

I and Albert, which played for a relatively short run at the Piccadilly in 1972, presented a series of quite magnificent stage pictures, both in the form of well-directed crowd scenes and by admirably controlled lighting and projections. In fact, with a good cast led by Polly James as Queen Victoria, and with good music by Charles Strause, it seemed to have the ingredients of success – but the subject defeated the efforts of the writer, Jay Allen, who simply could not with any conviction crowd the incidents of such a long life (the play covered the Queen's whole reign) into one evening.

One came away with some happy memories of particular scenes – of

Disraeli dancing a tango with a creaky Gladstone, for instance (and indeed Lewis Fiander stopped the show as Disraeli, the conjurer); but the play was a failure, after all.

Other worthy and unworthy failures crowded the late sixties and early seventies – *Man of Magic*, based on the life of Houdini; a musical version of Daisy Ashford's *The Young Visiters*; attempts to musicalise novels – *Two Cities* (from Dickens), *Ann Veronica* (from Wells), *Tom Brown's Schooldays* (from Hughes), *The Card* (from Bennett) and even *Mandrake* (from Machiavelli!). But these were beginning to look like the tattered remnants of a dying tradition. A new vogue, a new attitude to the musical, and above all a new musical taste, was taking over.

Envoi

The future of the British musical comedy or operetta might seem to be slender: in fact there are signs that it may be extremely happy, given that audiences are willing to accept changes in the *genre* as radical as those suggested in the forties by *Oklahoma!* Indeed, now that America has rejected experimentalism in the musical (in the shape of Stephen Sondheim's latest work), preferring the ultra-conventional, if extremely entertaining, form of *Chorus Line*, it may be that British composers have the opportunity to reassert a degree of leadership. The possible direction in which the light musical theatre may turn can perhaps be exemplified by two British musicals of the seventies – *The Rocky Horror Show* and *Jesus Christ Superstar*.

The Rocky Horror Show opened at the Theatre Upstairs – above the Royal Court Theatre in Sloane Square – on June 19, 1973, announced as 'a rock musical' with book and lyrics by Richard O'Brien. Greeted with enthusiasm by the critics and public, it transferred to the Classic Cinema in the King's Road, Chelsea, and then to another cinema, rechristened the King's Road Theatre, where it is still running at the time of writing. O'Brien conceived an evening which should provide on the one hand a splendid send-up of late-night horror movies (introduced, indeed, by an usherette singing of the joys of 'The Late Night Pitchur Show'), and on the other determined advocacy of sexual freedom. The story, such as it is, concerns Brad Majors and his naive girl-friend Janet Weiss, stranded late one night by a puncture and taking refuge in a macabre castle inhabited by Frank-n-Furter, a transsexual dressed in woman's underclothing (Tim Curry made a sensation in the part, and in the subsequent film) reigning over his entourage of genially terrifying servants, headed by Riff Raff, who resembles nothing so much as Toulouse Lautrec's drawing of the rubber-boned Valentin.

Frank-n-Furter has made – in the sense of creating, but also in every other sense – the handsome, body-building hero Rocky Horror, dressed in gold jockstrap and boots, his muscular body glittering with golddust. Brad and Janet are escorted through an entertainment during which both are sexually initiated by Frank-n-Furter, and are finally released from their sexual fears and tensions (which is good), while Frank-n-Furter and Rocky Horror end up dead (which is presumably also good).

Tim Curry (reclining) as Frank-n-Furter in Richard O'Brien's *The Rocky Horror Show* (1973) with Nell Campbell, Patricia Quinn and Richard O'Brien himself – a still from the film made of the stage production.

It cannot be said to be an evening of intellectual stimulation (and thus is right in the tradition of musical comedy!); but the book and what one can hear of the lyrics are intelligent and witty, and the music appealing, if unoriginal. The production and costumes, by Jim Sharman, Brian Thompson and Peter Walker, are innocently sexy and at the same time funny, and it would be an incorrigibly old-fashioned theatre-goer who would not find something to enjoy in the production.

Tim Rice

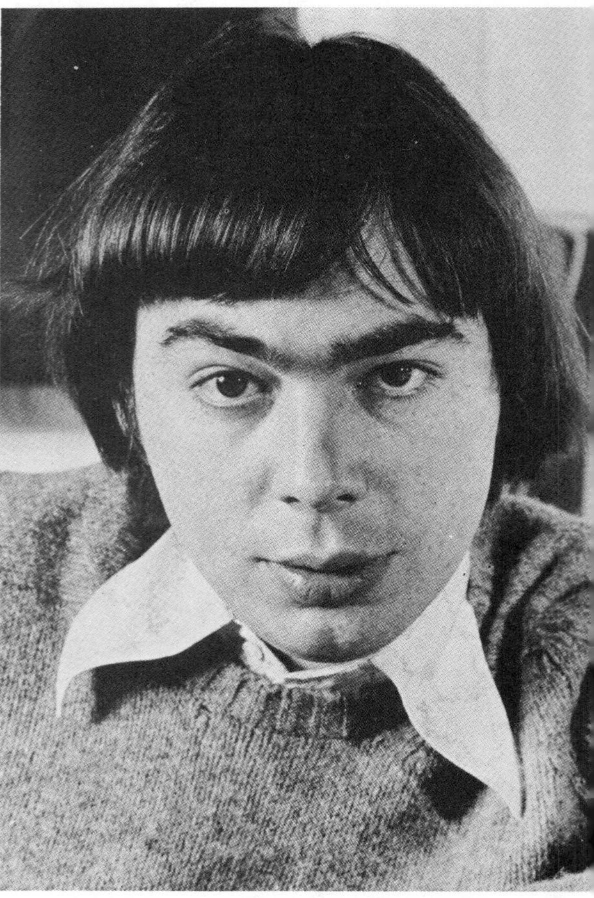

Andrew Lloyd-Webber

Andrew Lloyd-Webber and Tim Rice are, respectively, composer and librettist of the most successful British musical of post-war years. *Jesus Christ Superstar* caused controversy when first produced (1972), but few found its attitude to its subject in any sense irreligious.

In 1976, O'Brien, with a collaborator Richard Hartley (the original musical director of *The Rocky Horror Show*) tried to repeat the success with *T. Zee*, which played for a very short run at the Royal Court. Two anthropologists exploring the desert of Los Angeles, sometime in the future, are captured by Tarzan and a company of ghouls who carry them off through trapdoors to an underworld kingdom ruled by the pop-star sadist, Bone Idol, and his sexually insatiable consort, Princess La. Rock and country music introduce a variety of characters – former show-business lawyers, extras and television personalities – in a world of sexual fantasy in which only deviation is conventional. The show had enormous vitality, and was played with great verve; but the enthusiasm which carried *The Rocky Horror Show* along could not save an idea in which the main notion seemed to be to outrage an audience which, by its very presence, had already signalled that it was incapable of being outraged, and the joke was too thin.

The most outstanding musical play of the seventies is likely to be *Jesus Christ Superstar*, which opened at the Palace on August 9, 1972. It is a show particularly difficult to categorise: the composer and author, Andrew Lloyd-Webber and Tim Rice, described their other entertainment, *Joseph and the Amazing Technicolor Dreamcoat*, as 'a pop oratorio', and indeed there is a sense in which *Jesus Christ Superstar* is also an oratorio: the stage movement is on the whole superfluous – it is the score which matters.

Composer and librettist met in 1965, when Lloyd-Webber was seventeen and Rice twenty-one. The composer had been educated at Westminster School and Magdalen College, Oxford, which he left after only one term to concentrate on music. He published a piano suite which was written when he was only nine.

Rice was rather longer in declaring his talent. Educated at Lancing College and at the Sorbonne, he worked as both a law student and a petrol-pump attendant before joining E.M.I. Records, and then becoming a record producer on his own account. He and Lloyd-Webber planned at first an opera based on the life of Dr Barnardo, a few pop songs which failed to sell, and finally collaborated on *Joseph and the Amazing Technicolor Dreamcoat*, much performed in English and American schools.

Jesus Christ Superstar made its first appearance as a double gramophone record, and achieved great popularity in that form – it has sold over seven million copies. Its staging provided great problems, and was solved by setting the stage out as a simple rostrum – a flat acting area with two vertiginously-tilted platforms, one on each side, and spaces recessed into them for piano and organ/synthesizer on one side, and guitars (classical and rhythm) on the other. In the central space the 'story' is told in the simplest actions, while the chorus climbs the ramps and strides the platform above the central rostrum. One difficulty totally unsolved is that the score demands the microphones inseperable from contemporary rock music; this means that in the London production the actors spend much time passing a microphone from one to the other, totally abolishing any dramatic tension. This is obviously something that must be amended by technical means, if rock music is ever to survive stage presentation.

Having said that, there is no denying the power of the work. The score, written when Lloyd-Webber was in his early twenties, is of great richness, and marvellously well orchestrated not only for the apparatus of rock music, but a large string section: eight violins, two violas, two cellos, bass, woodwind, horns, trumpets, trombone and tuba. The result of this adventurous scoring is to give the musical texture of the piece an interest quite foreign to even the most ambitious contemporary musicals. The adventurousness of the orchestration is not always matched by the quality of the music itself; the title-piece relies for its effect on the repetition of one simple, short theme. But some other numbers are indeed memorable : Mary's song, 'I Don't Know How to Love Him' has been recorded by over fifty different artistes; 'Hosanna Heysanna Sanna Sanna Ho' is a chorus of splendid gaiety, and becomes dreadfully ironical in its reprise during the short scene between Christ and Pilate; and there is the wonderfully dramatic razmataz song for King Herod – again, most imaginatively scored – which is at the nasty centre of the scene of the degradation of Christ.

If at the very end, giving the penultimate music to strings alone, and in uninspired bars which recall Victorian sentimental church music, Mr Lloyd-Webber loses his nerve, the piece as a whole is a considerable achievement in popular stage music.

As librettist, Tim Rice faced several difficult problems (*Jesus Christ Superstar* has no spoken dialogue at all, and little 'recitative'; the piece is one long series of major numbers). Like many libretti, this one does not bear reading very well, though where he can the librettist makes his points with incisive wit – as, again, in Herod's song:

> Jesus you won't believe the hit you've made
> round here
> You are all we talk about the wonder of the
> year
> Oh what a pity if it's all a lie
> Still I'm sure that you can rock the cynics if
> you try
>
> So you are the Christ you're the great Jesus Christ
> Prove to me that you're no fool walk across my
> swimming pool
> If you do that for me then I'll let you go free
> C'mon King of the Jews . . .

Jeeves, a musical based on the short stories and novels of P. G. Wodehouse, had Lloyd-Webber's music to a book by Alan Ayckbourn, and played briefly at Her Majesty's in 1975 with a spectacularly good cast; but it proved, like *Twang!!,* an almost complete failure. *Evita,* in which Lloyd-Webber was again joined by Tim Rice, was first produced as a recording in 1976, and showed an enormous technical advance on their earlier work.

The recording allowed the composer to score for an enormous cast of soloists and choristers, rock musicians and the London Philharmonia

Steve Alder as Jesus of Nazareth and Sharon Campbell as Mary Magdalene in Andrew Lloyd-Webber and Tim Rice's *Jesus Christ Superstar*, in its fifth year at the Palace Theatre, London.

Orchestra; it took six months to make, and cost £90,000. A stage production followed at the Prince Edward Theatre (formerly The London Casino) in 1978.

Setting to music a loosely-narrated and episodic biography of Eva Peron, the mistress and later the wife of the President and dictator of Argentina, the composer and librettist deliberately attempted to widen their scope with *Evita,* which explores a complex personality made somewhat more complex by Tim Rice's successful attempt to show her not as the 'local girl makes good' of many show-business musicals, but as a woman involved in corruption as well as charity, fascist politics as well as go-getting.

The first few minutes of the score demonstrate, especially in Lloyd-Webber's original orchestration (somewhat modified for the smaller forces in the theatre, where there is tactful re-scoring by Hershy Kay) the musical breadth of the work. Choral writing for the mourning crowd at Eva's funeral reminds one as much of the work of Penderecki as anyone else, and is backed by instrumentation with an Indian flavour. Then sweeps in a full complement of strings in a Tchaikowskian treatment of one of the musical's main themes. Tschaikowsky and Penderecki co-exist for a few bars before being overtaken by a Latin-American number for Che, the wry satirical commentator on the story. Splendidly, the original theme of this number turns into the melody of Evita's heavily-plugged main theme, 'Don't Cry for Me, Argentina', before the chorus enters again with 'Salve regina mater misericordia . . . ' Lloyd-Webber certainly has a talent for melody, which is shown in *Evita* much more obviously than in *Superstar:* 'Don't Cry for Me, Argentina' is only one example, and 'High Flying, Adored' another; then there are the edgy, satirical numbers like the 'Waltz for Eva and Che'.

The stage production opened on June 21, 1978, after an enormous amount of bally-hoo, and immediately justified the publicity by the spectacularly inventive direction of Harold Prince, and the performances of David Essex (as Che, sung on the recording by C. T. Wilkinson), Elaine Paige (replacing the recorded Evita of Julie Covington), and Joss Ackland (Paul Jones). It was widely praised, in some cases perhaps overpraised: Derek Jewell in *The Sunday Times* has called it 'quite simply a masterpiece . . . the best tunes are tremendous. Lloyd-Webber's score is, in beauty and dramatic impact, overwhelming.' Perhaps one should make allowances for a critic more used to light music than classical opera, and evidently somewhat overcome to find a composer who can write rock yet score for a symphony orchestra.

Evita, an extremely costly production, announces a new vein in the *genre* which is difficult to define. Lloyd-Webber is certainly not writing opera, as some critics have claimed; but he is much nearer the idiom of Bernstein than of Bart, obviously, and audiences for *Evita* have to work harder to comprehend the music they are being offered than has commonly been the rule in musical comedy. One thing is clear: exploration will continue, and the composer and writer who have so energetically burst out of the straitjacket which contained the *genre* for so long will be watched closely over the next decade or so. If 'the musical' is going anywhere of interest, it will surely be along the route they are pioneering.

The Top Ten Long-Running British Musicals

Jesus Christ, Super-Star	2620 performances*
Oliver!	2618 performances†
Salad Days	2283 performances
Chu Chin Chow	2238 performances
Charlie Girl	2202 performances
The Boy Friend	2084 performances
Canterbury Tales	2082 performances
Me and My Girl	1646 performances
The Maid of the Mountains	1352 performances
Perchance to Dream	1022 performances

*as on October 3, 1978
†not including performances of the 1977 revival

Bibliography

Agate, James: *At Half Past Eight* (Cape, 1923)
The Contemporary Theatre 1923 (Chapman and Hall, 1924)
The Contemporary Theatre 1924 (Chapman and Hall, 1925)
The Contemporary Theatre 1925 (Chapman and Hall, 1926)
The Contemporary Theatre 1926 (Chapman and Hall, 1927)
The Contemporary Theatre 1944-5 (Chapman and Hall, 1946)
First Nights (Nicolson & Watson, 1934)
The Amazing Theatre (Harrap, 1939)
Egos 1-9 (Harrap, 1938-47)

Asche, Oscar: *Oscar Asche, His Life* (Hurst & Blackett, 1929)

Barker, Felix: *The House that Stoll Built* (Frederick Muller, 1959)

Cochran, C. B.: *Cock-a-Doodle-Doo* (J. M. Dent, 1941)
A Showman Looks On (J. M. Dent, 1945)

Curtis, Anthony: (ed.) *The Rise and Fall of the Matinée Idol* (Weidenfeld & Nicolson, 1974)

Dean, Basil: *The Theatre at War* (Harrap, 1956)
Hind's Eye (Hutchinson, 1973)

Dunhill, Thomas: *Sullivan's Comic Operas* (Edward Arnold, 1931)

Ellis, Vivian: *I'm on a See-Saw* (Michael Joseph, 1953)

Forbes-Winslow, D.: *Daly's* (W. H. Allen, 1944)

Graves, George: *Gaieties and Gravities* (Hutchinson, 1931)

Grossmith, George: *G. G.* (Hutchinson, 1933)

Henson, Leslie: *Yours Faithfully* (Harrap, 1948)

Herbert, Alan: *A.P.H.* (Heinemann, 1970)

Hughes, Gervase: *Composers of Operetta* (Macmillan, 1962)

Hulbert, Jack: *The Little Woman's Always Right* (W. H. Allen, 1975)

Kennedy, Michael: *The Works of R. Vaughan Williams* (Oxford University Press, 1964)

Lesley, Cole: *The Life of Noël Coward* (Jonathan Cape, 1976)

Lupino, Stanley: *From the Stocks to the Stars* (Hutchinson, 1934)

Mackinlay, Stirling: *The Origin and Development of Light Opera* (Hutchinson, 1928)

Mander, Raymond and Mitchenson, Joe: *Musical Comedy* (Peter Davies, 1969)

Theatrical Companion to Noël Coward (Rockliff, 1957)

Maschwitz, Eric: *No Chip on my Shoulder* (W. H. Allen, 1964)

Morley, Sheridan: *A Talent to Amuse* (Heinemann, 1969)

Parker, Derek and Julia: *The Natural History of the Chorus Girl* (David & Charles, 1975)

Macqueen Pope, W.: *Gaiety, Theatre of Enchantment* (W. H. Allen, 1949)

Ivor (W. H. Allen, 1950)

The Footlights Flickered (Herbert Jenkins, 1959)

Nights of Gladness (Hutchinson, 1956)

Short, Ernest: *Sixty Years of Theatre* (Eyre & Spottiswode, 1946)

Smyth, Ethel: *A Final Burning of Boats* (Longmans, Green, 1928)

White, Eric Walter: *The Rise of English Opera* (John Lehmann, 1951)

Wilson, Sandy: *I Could be Happy* (Michael Joseph, 1975)

Ivor Novello (Michael Joseph)

Wodehouse, P. G.: *Performing Flea* (Herbert Jenkins, 1953)

Who's Who in the Theatre (Editions 1-15) (J. M. Pitman)
The Times, *The Daily Telegraph*, *The Stage*, *The Illustrated London News*, *Punch* and other journals.

Chronological Index of Musical Plays

Productions mentioned in this book are listed under the year of first production, and in alphabetical order. The page-numbers given are of the major references.

Chronological Index of Musical Plays

Index of Musical Plays

Incorporating burlesques, revues, musical comedies, operettas, comic operas and operas. Figures in bold type indicate illustrations, "ff" stands for following pages.

General Index

Figures in bold type indicate illustrations, ff stands for following pages.

Printed by Clarke, Doble & Brendon Ltd., Plymouth